# Case Book

to accompany

# E-commerce

business. technology. society.

Second Edition

## Kenneth C. Laudon

## Carol Guercio Traver

PEARSON

Addison
Wesley

Boston  San Francisco  New York
London  Toronto  Sydney  Tokyo  Singapore  Madrid
Mexico City  Munich  Paris  Cape Town  Hong Kong  Montreal

| | |
|---|---|
| Executive Editor | Susan Hartman Sullivan |
| Assistant Editor | Elizabeth Paquin |
| Marketing Manager | Michelle Brown |
| Senior Production Supervisor | Jeffrey Holcomb |
| Project Management | Meghan James |
| Composition | Laura Wiegleb |
| Text Designer | Geri Davis |
| Cover Designer | Joyce Cosentino Wells |
| Prepress and Manufacturing | Caroline Fell |

Access the latest information about Addison-Wesley titles from our World Wide Web site: http://www.aw-bc.com/computing

ISBN 0-321-26936-5

1 2 3 4 5-CRS-06 05 04

PEARSON

Addison
Wesley

# TABLE OF CONTENTS

**MARKETING CASE STUDIES**

**E-COMMERCE IN ACTION**

# PREFACE

*E-Commerce: Case Book* is a collection of new, in-depth cases intended to supplement the text *E-Commerce: Business, Technology, Society, Second Edition*. There are five marketing cases that focus on topics in marketing principles and marketing communications. These are followed by five new E-commerce in Action cases that focus on five e-commerce sectors: retail, services, B2B, auctions/portals/communities, and digital content. The E-commerce in Action cases focus on entrepreneurial vision, Internet strategy, business model evolution, and financial performance. Both types of cases parallel the style of analysis used in the book for in-depth end-of-chapter cases and E-commerce in Action cases. The cases are organized within this supplemental case book in a manner that reflects the Table of Contents for the textbook. Below we describe briefly the content of each case and the textbook chapter it is intended to support.

## E-Commerce Marketing Case Studies

### Case 1: Procter & Gamble: Two Moments of Truth in the Age of the Internet.

This case describes the efforts of Procter & Gamble to use the Internet to build direct relationships with its consumers and yet avoid competing with its primary distribution channel owners such as Wal-Mart and other large national retailers. Management has decided not to follow a direct-to-consumer strategy like Dell, but rather to develop "product communities." New CEO Alan Lafley has focused his Internet strategy on what P & G terms the "consumer moments of truth: the decision to purchase a P&G product, and the consumer's experience in using the product for the first time. Designed to support Chapter 7, E-Commerce Marketing Concepts.

### Case 2: Avon Calling: A "Rep-Centric" Web Marketing Model.

This case describes the strategies pursued by Avon in re-intermediating its primary direct sales force. The case recounts how Avon flirted with the idea of pursuing a direct sales Internet model, and then realized that its greatest asset was its nearly 4 million person direct sales force. The problem was how to use the Internet to strengthen this traditional face-to-face sales force, develop a direct sales channel, and re-position the company's products and channels to appeal to a younger Internet-savvy generation of women. Avon management is attempting to use the Internet as a lever for transforming the business processes of its sales force rather than replacing the sales force. Designed to support Chapter 7, E-Commerce Marketing Concepts.

### Case 3: Reed Elsevier Internet Marketing Strategy: Digital Bundling and "The Big Deal" Drive Net Profits but Rouse Opposition.

Reed Elsevier is the world's leading publisher of science, technology and medical journals. A traditional publishing company founded in the 19th century, Reed Elsevier developed a digital platform called ScienceDirect for the distribution of scientific journals to universities worldwide. ScienceDirect bundles hundreds of journals into a single "Big Deal" package for which universities pay a single price. In the pursuit of double-digit profit growth, Reed Elsevier has unleashed a torrent of consumer resistance to its pricing strategy. University professors, researchers, and administrators are pressuring Reed Elsevier to unbundle its offering and drop prices. Worse, they are attempting to build online scientific journals that are "free." Designed to support Chapter 7, E-Commerce Marketing Concepts.

### Case 4: Advergames: Engage Your Customer, Get Personal, Make a Sale, Have Fun.

This case describes advergames, one of the fastest growing forms of online advertising. Advergames combine online games with advertising in several ways. Generally, marketers build a new game around a product in an effort to attract consumers and increase brand awareness. The concepts of relationship marketing, awareness marketing, transactional marketing and consultative marketing are reviewed. Advergames are a type of relationship marketing which attempt to build a personal and customized relationship with each consumer. Compared to other forms of marketing communications, advergames are highly interactive, causing online consumers to pause and linger at a site playing the game. Advergame vendors claim this form of advertising produces high levels of brand awareness and loyalty. Designed to support Chapter 8, E-Commerce Marketing Communications.

### Case 5: Internet Advertising Movies: We Interrupt This E-mail to Bring You an Important Video From Your Sponsor.

This case chronicles the rise of online video advertising, or the use of television-like commercials, as a form of marketing communications. Online video advertising appears at a time when consumer resistance to direct e-mail and pop-up/pop-under advertising is growing very rapidly, leading to legislation and counter-advertising software. Online portals have responded by developing anti-spam and pop-up blocking software. Online video advertising offers consumers and advertisers several advantages. However, if the advertising industry is unable to exercise restraint, and if online video advertising becomes intrusive and de-personalizing like e-mail and pop-up advertising, then this new form of advertising may suffer the same fate as direct e-mail marketing and pop-up ads. Designed to support Chapter 8, E-Commerce Marketing Communications and Chapter 9, Ethical, Social and Political Issues in E-Commerce.

## E-Commerce in Action Case Studies

### Case 6: RedEnvelope: Unique Gifts in Short Supply.

RedEnvelope is an entrepreneurial Web-based start up in the retail business of providing customers with truly unique gifts that are unavailable elsewhere in retail stores or on the Web. The case describes the growth of the company since 1997 to its current size of about $70 million in revenue. During this period, the company has had to develop scale economies at its distribution center, develop a compelling Web site that would help consumers solve "gifting occasion" dilemmas, and develop a supply chain that could reliably deliver unique gifts. The company has demonstrated strong revenue growth in the past years, and an improving financial performance. But new competitors threaten the company's dominance in the gifting marketplace, and its supply chain has been unable to keep up with demand. Designed to support Chapter 10, Retailing on the Web.

### Case 7: InsWeb and the Online Insurance Market.

This case chronicles the evolution of the online insurance market, and the efforts of one of the largest online insurance services, InsWeb.com. InsWeb began in 1995 as an online insurance intermediary steering online consumers to traditional insurance companies for a fee. But as traditional insurance companies developed their own online capabilities, and larger financial institutions began offering insurance at their integrated sites, InsWeb and other similar intermediaries have had to evolve their business model. InsWeb is seeking to offer insurance directly to some consumers and is considering transforming itself into an insurance "super agency" competing directly with local insurance agents. Designed to support Chapter 11, Online Service Industries.

### Case 8: WebMD: Rx for the Nation's Medical Ills.

This case describes the growth of WebMD (formerly Healtheon) into the nation's largest online medical services company. While the company is best known for its popular online consumer-oriented WebMD.com site that provides medical information to consumers, most of its revenues derive from the electronic data interchange (EDI) services it provides to medical providers (doctors) and insurers, including the federal government. Management believes that new legislation (HIPAA, the Health Insurance Portability and Accountability Act of 1996) will cause more health institutions to adopt a form of digital medical record and more standardized B2B documents for the health industry. However, it is unclear if WebMD can benefit from this transition to digital medical records and transactions. Designed to support Chapter 12, B2B E-Commerce: Supply Chain Management and Collaborative Commerce.

### Case 9: Ask Jeeves: The Butler Knows.

The Ask Jeeves case describes the development and growth trajectory of the 5th largest search engine on the Internet, with about $77 million in revenue for 2003. Ask Jeeves has shown erratic revenue growth, but it nevertheless has slowly reduced its losses and in 2003 showed its first profit ever. While focusing on the individual consumer search market, the company's original branded search product has been surpassed by other pure search engines such as Google. Moreover, Ask Jeeves does not offer consumers content like Yahoo! or MSN. In a period of industry consolidation and alliances, it is unclear if a pure search engine can survive as an independent firm. Management is attempting to focus the company's efforts by selling off divisions, and re-building the search engine to gain a technological edge over competitors. Designed to support Chapter 13, Auctions, Portals and Communities

**Case 10: RealNetworks: Media Player to Media Portal.**

RealNetworks is a pioneer in the development of online media players for the Internet, beginning with RealAudio in 1994. Today RealNetworks is a $200 million company based on sales of its RealOne media player and a growing online music subscription service. In fact, RealNetworks is the most successful online music subscription service. But competition in this space is growing even though the subscription model is more profitable than the single-song, retail model of Apple Computer's iTunes site. Moreover, RealNetworks is locked into a head-to-head competition with Microsoft and its MediaPlayer. Microsoft continues to bundle its MediaPlayer with its Windows operating system in the U.S. and elsewhere, and RealNetworks continues to push government anti-trust authorities in the U.S. and Europe for relief. Few companies win competitions with Microsoft. The challenge facing RealNetwork's management is how to achieve profitability in a world dominated by Microsoft's operating system and its bundled media player. Designed to support Chapter 14, Online Digital Content Providers: Digital Media.

# MARKETING CASE STUDIES

# Procter & Gamble:

## Two Moments of Truth in the Age of the Internet

How can a mature consumer products company use the Internet to revive stagnant brand sales, invigorate product development, and develop online marketing programs to accelerate sales of its traditional brands? How does a global mass retailer comfortable with selling to millions of consumers through large-scale national retailers such as Wal-Mart use the Web to build a personal relationship with customers, and even personalize its products? Procter & Gamble offers some interesting answers to these questions.

For most of its 166 years, P&G has been one of America's preeminent companies. The company's three largest brands are Tide, Pampers, and Crest—each garnering well over $1 billion in annual sales, as do ten other P&G brands. P&G's brands are national and even global icons. P&G launched Tide in 1946, in 1960 won American Dental Association approval for Crest toothpaste as an effective cavity fighter, and in 1961, it rolled out Pampers—the first disposable diaper. In 1986 it launched Pert Plus, the first shampoo with a built-in conditioner.

P&G has a long history of inventing new marketing and branding tools. Some even say that P&G wrote the marketing handbook. In the 1880s, P&G was one of the first companies to advertise nationally through print ads in local newspapers. Fifty years later, in 1931, P&G harnessed the marketing power of a new technology called radio to pitch its cleaning products. It began to sponsor serial radio shows such as *Ma Perkins* and *Guiding Light*, which, because they were sponsored by the "soap" company P&G, came to be known as "soap operas." Currently, P&G spends more on advertising around the world than any other corporation on earth.

P&G's management techniques, meanwhile, became the gold standard. In the 1930s, P&G developed the concept of brand management—setting up marketing teams for each brand and urging them to compete against each other. P&G has long been the business world's finest management training ground. General Electric's Jeffrey R. Immelt and 3M's W. James McNerney, Jr. both started out with Ivory. Meg Whitman and Steven M. Case were in toilet goods, while Steven A. Ballmer was an assistant product manager for Duncan Hines cake mix, among other goods. They, of course, went on to lead eBay, AOL Time Warner, and Microsoft, respectively.

| **TABLE 1-1** | **P&G Brands** | | |
|---|---|---|---|
| A Touch of Sun | Dreft | Ivory Soap | Pert Plus |
| Actonel | Dryel | Joy | Physique |
| Always | Era | Loving Care | Prilosec OTC |
| Asacol | Eukanuba | Luvs | Pringles |
| Aussie | Febreze | Macrobid | Puffs |
| Balsam Color | Fixodent | Macrodantin | PUR |
| Bounce | Folgers | Max Factor | Safegfuard |
| Bounty | Gain | Men's Choice | Salvo |
| Camay | Giorgio Beverly Hills | Metamucil | Scope |
| Cascade | Gleem | Millstone | Secret |
| Charmin | Glide Dental Floss | Miss Clairol | Sunny Delight |
| Cheer | Head and Shoulders | Mr. Clean | Sure |
| Clairol | Helmut Lang | Natural Instincts | Swiffer |
| CoverGirl | Herbal Essences | Nice 'n' Easy | Tampax |
| Crest | Herve Leger | Noxzema | Thermacare |
| Daily Defense | Hugo Boss | Ohm by Olay | Tide |
| Dantrium | Hydrience | Olay | Torengos |
| Dantrium IV | Iams | Old Spice | Ultress |
| Dawn | Infusium 23 | Pampers | Vicks |
| Didronel | Ivory Dish | Pantene | Vidal Sassoon |
| Downy | Ivory Snow | Pepto-Bismol | Zest |

Today P&G is the world's largest consumer products company, with $43.3 billion in revenues, net profits of $5.1 billion, and operations in 78 countries. Every day in the United States, nearly every adult citizen is in close contact with one or more of the company's 84 brands (Table 1-1).

P&G's four core categories—fabric care, hair care, baby care, and feminine care—account for nearly 50% of sales and an even greater percentage of profit. The company's core strengths are branding, new product innovation, and global operations. P&G is one of the world's most successful brand-creation and brand-building companies, with 13 brands now selling more than $1 billion a year. P&G employs over 7,500 research scientists and PhDs engaged in product development in 20 research centers around the world.

P&G's current strategy is to grow organically without acquisitions, by strengthening market penetration of its key brands and extending its existing brands to new products. A second strategy is to grow faster by strengthening its relationships with leading national retailers such as Wal-Mart, Target, JC Penney, and Sears. In the United States, the top ten retailers have increased their share of the market from 30% to 55% in the past five years as consumers flocked to large discount national chain stores. A third strategic objective is to develop and invest in faster-growing, higher-margin businesses such as health care and beauty care, which have much higher margins than traditional soap products. Today P&G has $5 billion health and beauty brands. The acquisition of Wella health and beauty care products in 2002 added a sixth.

## THE EARLY INTERNET ERA

When the Internet and Web first began to expand into a viable commercial channel, P&G was not well prepared. In the late 1990s, P&G was in danger of becoming another Eastman Kodak or Xerox, both great companies that had lost their way. Sales of most of P&G's 18 top brands were slowing; the company was being outhustled by more focused rivals such as Kimberly-Clark and Colgate-Palmolive. P&G hadn't created a successful new product in a decade. In the late 1990s, the only way P&G kept profits growing was by cutting costs, hardly a strategy for the long term. At the same time, the dynamics of the industry were changing, as power shifted from manufacturers to massive retailers such as Wal-Mart and Target. Through all this, much of P&G's senior management was in denial. "Nobody wanted to talk about it," the current CEO, A. G. Lafley, says. Stock prices for the company used to be in the $130 range but fell to the $55 range in 1999 as investors became more and more disappointed with failed earnings forecasts, lack of innovation, and an insular corporate culture that was routinely compared to a fortress built to oppose change.

## MANUFACTURERS IN THE AGE OF THE INTERNET

How were manufacturers supposed to take advantage of the Internet? According to the popular wisdom of the day, it was expected that manufacturers would develop a direct sales relationship with the consumer, using the Internet as a virtual storefront and offer consumers lower prices. But this model did not work for manufacturers of automobiles, consumer durables such as appliances, and furniture. Most manufacturers historically relied on distributors, registered dealerships, and large national retail stores to develop a direct, personal relationship with the customer, make the presentation, book the sale, deliver the goods, and support the product after the sale. The few exceptions, such as Dell, never had a powerful national distribution channel and simply segued their direct marketing techniques developed in the age of the telephone to the new Internet channel. But for most manufacturers dependent on wholesale and retail distributors, how to use the Internet was a bit of a quandary. Until a new CEO arrived in 2000, P&G, like many manufacturers, did not have a Web strategy.

## DEVELOPING A WEB BRANDING STRATEGY

All this changed in June 2000, when Alan G. Lafley was appointed CEO. Lafley has led a turnaround that has exceeded most forecasts. Lafley restructured the company's brands, selling off poor margin brands and purchasing brands such as Clairol. Laying off over 9,000 workers in 2001 also helped the bottom line, but it did not help the top line. P&G has not developed a major blockbuster brand like Tide or Pampers or Crest in the last 20 years. Instead, the company has done a better job of extending its existing brands. In the case of Crest, for instance, it created the Crest Spin Brush teethcleaning tool (spinbrush.com), Crest White Strips, and a teeth maintenance product called MultiCare. P&G is also experimenting with Reflect.com, its customized online cosmetics business, whose main benefit to date appears to be research.

As a result of these efforts, analysts expect P&G to post a 13% increase in net income on 8% higher sales for the fiscal year ending June 30, 2004. That would bring P&G's annual compounded earnings growth rate under the three years of Lafley's leadership to 15%—a rate well above rivals. During that period, P&G's stock price has climbed by 58%, while the Standard & Poor 500 stock index fell by 32% (P&G's stock has recently traded at $100).

Effective use of the Internet has been a cornerstone of Lafley's turnaround effort. More so than rivals Unilever and Colgate-Palmolive, P&G has been treading the boundaries between old and new, traditional core money-makers and forward-thinking new ventures. By experimenting with new ways to increase revenue, the once overly conservative giant is now in the position of selling unused patents and leasing its marketing and technological expertise to other companies (yet2.com).

## THE TWO MARKETING MOMENTS OF TRUTH

Lafley was made CEO in 2000 following a disastrous 18-month period when the previous CEO tried to orchestrate change from above and grew earnings by firing staff and reducing costs, allowing new product development to stagnate. Lafley's goal is to make P&G into a svelte Web-enabled profit-producing machine. Lafley points to the two marketing moments of truth as the moments that all P&G employees need to focus on. The first moment of truth is when the consumer decides to buy a P&G product. The second moment of truth occurs when the consumer tries the product for the first time. Thirty million times each day a consumer looks at a P&G product—then either buys it or buys the competing product. That works out to more than a million moments of truth an hour. Each day about 1 million consumers try a P&G product for the first time, generating another 40,000 moments of truth each hour. One of Lafley's goals is to build a marketing

and branding machine that can understand these moments and build products that consumers want to purchase and use.

The question is, "How can P&G use the Internet to influence these moments of truth in favor of P&G products?"

Lafley realized that P&G could no longer rely on strategic partners to provide this information, nor could it rely on mass-marketing techniques to promote its products or on traditional focus groups to find out how consumers feel about products. Instead, Lafley has attempted to use the Web not as a direct sales channel but rather as a channel to develop a new, more intimate relationship with P&G customers in order to come up with new product ideas, test new products, and obtain feedback on existing products. In the process, P&G is once again redefining how brands are launched, nurtured, promoted, and sold in the United States and the world.

## THE ROLE OF THE WEB IN P&G'S TRANSFORMATION

Table 1-2 illustrates the kinds of Web sites P&G has created in order to build this more intimate relationship with the consumer. The table does not include all of P&G's Web sites because it would be too lengthy for this case. In essence,

**TABLE 1-2**

| General Portal | |
| --- | --- |
| PG.com | Main corporate P&G site used to promote the main brands, announce new products, offer discounts, refer sales to local retailers. No direct sales. |
| **Existing Product Promotion** | |
| MrClean.com | Articles, special promotions, newsletters, related products, consumer polls, e-mail registration, registered memberships. |
| Tide.Com | |
| Olay.com | |
| Crest.com | |
| [79 other product-specific Web sites] | |
| **Direct Sales and Innovation** | |
| Reflect.com | Offers personalized cosmetics and personalized consumer-branding choices to upscale women. Joint venture with venture firms RedPoint Ventures and Institutional Venture Partners. Used for developing a trusted relationship with an upscale audience. Direct sales. |
| **New Product Development** | |
| Yet2.com | B2B auction site for P&G's and 40 other large companies' patents for ideas not yet developed. |
| **B2B Channel Management** | |
| Transora | B2B site that promotes and sells a data synchronization network and related tools to coordinate the flow of information among manufacturers and retailers worldwide. |

P&G has created a Web site for every one of its 84 brands and additional Web sites for other purposes. Table 1-2 classifies the sites into five different groups: general portal, existing product promotion, direct sales and innovation, new product development, and industry B2B channel management (focused on data exchanges). At each of the consumer-oriented sites, the idea is to build a participatory environment where consumers can have an impact on product design, provide feedback on the existing products, and register to receive more personalized mail messages about the product. These sites are in essence "product communities." For instance, on its Tide.com Web site, consumers find articles on stains and their removal, special offers, newsletters, consumer polls, e-mail sign-up opportunities for more regular product news, and registered memberships at the site.

To introduce a new hair care brand called Physique, P&G created a new Web site called physique.com and then handed out the URL on millions of restaurant napkins, coasters, and glasses in bars around the country. The result was 5 million hits in which consumers exchanged information about themselves in return for product samples.

## AVOIDING DIRECT-SELLING CONSUMER RELATIONSHIPS

In general, P&G has avoided direct-selling relationships with the consumer and instead has focused on helping consumers understand how to use the product. The only exception has been when a new product is introduced (such as Crest teeth-whitening strips) or when a new product is offered exclusively over the Web and probably could not be offered at a traditional mass retailer. For instance, the Reflect.com site permits consumers to create custom cosmetics that are not and never have been available through retail channels.

# P&G'S WEB STRATEGY

Although P&G was late in learning how to use the Web, since 2000 it has made up for lost time. Currently it uses the Web to build stronger, more intimate relationships with customers without alienating the large mass retailers that constitute its sole retail outlet. Contrary to early speculation on e-commerce, P&G has avoided developing direct-selling relationships with the consumer but rather uses the Web to drive consumers to its traditional retailing partners. By maintaining its powerful brand image, P&G has so far been able to prevent large retailers such as Wal-Mart and Walgreens from developing their own house-branded lines of health, hair, beauty, and skin products. Even though some mass retailers indeed have developed house brands that sell for a fraction of P&G's retail prices, most consumers at the moment of truth still reach for the P&G brand that they read about in newspaper ads, see on television soap operas, and increasingly see on the Web.

## SOURCES

Berner, Robert. "The P&G Revolution." *BusinessWeek*, July 7, 2003.

Ellison, Sarah. "In Lean Times, Big Companies Make a Grab for Market Share." *Wall Street Journal*, September 5, 2003.

Helmke, Kathryn. "CEO talks about principles that saved Procter & Gamble." *Naples Daily News*, February 14, 2004.

Procter and Gamble Company Annual Report, 2003, www.pg.com.

Procter and Gamble Company Form 10-Q for the period ending September 30, 2003, filed with the Securities and Exchange Commission on October 30, 2003.

"Procter & Gamble Ups Guidance." TheStreet.com, March 9, 2004.

Stahl, Stephanie, and John Soat. "Feeding the Pipeline." *Informationweek*, February 24, 2003.

# Avon Calling:

## A "Rep-Centric" Web Marketing Model

When the doorbell rings, millions of women around the world are not surprised to hear the Avon mantra "Avon Calling." The question facing Avon management is how to translate this 100-year-old mantra onto the Internet.

Avon Products Inc., with world head-quarters in New York, has been selling through a direct sales force to households since 1885. Today, 98% of its $6 billion in sales worldwide comes through its direct sales force. Avon is one of the world's largest man-ufacturers and marketers of beauty and beauty-related products. Avon currently has operations in 58 countries, including the United States, and its products are distributed in 72 more, for coverage in 130 markets. Its two newest markets are Bosnia and Kazakhstan, both added in 2003. Sales are made to the ultimate customer principally through a combination of direct selling and marketing by approximately 3.9 million active independent Avon Representatives, approximately 570,000 of whom are in the United States and the rest in Europe, Asia, and Latin America. In 2003, Avon generated revenues of $6.8 billion, of which $2.2 billion was generated in the United States. By most measures, Avon is the global model for how to successfully run a direct sales force over a long period of time.

Avon's products fall into four product categories: Beauty, which consists of cosmetics, fragrances, and toiletries; Beauty Plus, which consists of jewelry, watches, apparel, and accessories; Beyond Beauty, which consists of home products, gifts, decorative products, and candles; and Health and Wellness, which consists of vitamins, an aromatherapy line, exercise equipment, stress relief, and weight management products.

Avon experienced single-digit growth throughout the 1990s as the average age of Avon customers increased. In the United States, Avon also faced a powerful demographic trend: women were increasingly at work and less likely to be at home to receive an Avon sales representative. Avon did not have strong sales to the fast-growing, coveted demographic groups of teenage girls (renowned for their purchases of cosmetics) or working women in the 21-to-45 age bracket, who account for more than 75% of all cosmetics sales in the United States.

## MANAGEMENT STRATEGIES FOR DOUBLE-DIGIT GROWTH: 1997–2004

With a lagging stock price and criticism from Wall Street investors seeking rapid stock price appreciation in the middle of the Internet stock bubble, Avon management launched a series of efforts they called the "Business Transformation Program" in the late 1990s in an attempt to pump up Avon's revenue growth and earnings into the double-digit column.

The first effort involved changing the brand image of Avon by creating new products and new retail physical store outlets to sell the new products directly to younger and working women who shopped in malls and department stores. The second major effort involved transforming the direct sales channel either by eliminating it completely and selling directly over the Internet to "the new woman" or integrating the Internet somehow into the overall channel mix. In the late 1990s, no one knew exactly how the Internet could be integrated into the channel mix without alienating the traditional direct sales force, most of whom did not even own a computer let alone have Web access.

# NEW PRODUCTS, NEW CHANNELS: BECOMING AND MARK

In 2000, Avon began development of a new brand called beComing. In 2001, the brand was launched with JC Penney as the main distribution channel. Avon offered the same line to Sears but was refused. The beComing line was aimed at teenagers and young women in the 16– to 24–year-old range who mostly associated the name Avon with their mothers. There are 17 million women in this age group in the United States with an aggregate purchasing power of $96 billion, one quarter of which is spent on beauty and beauty-related products. This group tends to shop at shopping malls, and the products were intended to be sold at exclusive counters in JC Penney stores by store sales personnel who had received special training. Unfortunately, the line did not do well. It was carried in only 90 Penney stores. In January 2003, Avon announced that it had agreed with JC Penney to end the business relationship. The beComing brand continues and is sold through Avon's direct sales channel in the United States exclusively by Avon beauty advisors, who are independent Avon sales representatives with specialized beauty product training and consultative selling skills.

In 2002, Avon began planning an entirely new global cosmetics brand named "mark," aimed at the 16-to-24 age group. In 2003, Avon launched mark. The product line is targeted to young women in the 16-to-24 age group, with the objective of enhancing Avon's share of the worldwide youth market. The new line was launched in fall 2003 in the United States and will roll out to Mexico and Brazil in 2004. The mark brand is being sold through both the company's core direct selling channel of U.S. representatives and a separate mark sales force. In Latin America and China, the new line will be sold through neighborhood kiosks and Avon retail stores, which have been a part of Avon's marketing channel mix in non-U.S. markets. The mark product line is too new to evaluate its impact on Avon's revenues.

# AVON'S DIRECT SALES FORCE IN THE AGE OF THE INTERNET

What makes Avon such an effective sales organization is a highly motivated direct sales force composed almost entirely of women who call on potential customers—generally friends and relatives—in their homes. Sales reps are taught how to mine their existing social and community relationships to sell Avon products. In a sense, the customers have already been acquired by Avon reps before the reps even join the sales program. Customer acquisition costs are therefore low. Acquiring customers for Avon is a process therefore of acquiring sales reps, and here the costs are higher and the churn or turnover of sales reps is also high. Nevertheless, executives came to realize in 2000 that the core asset of the company was its 3.9 million sales reps.

Representatives are independent contractors or independent dealers, who are not agents or employees of Avon. Representatives purchase products directly from Avon and sell them to their customers. The representatives are the customers of Avon, and Avon generally has no arrangement with any end user of its product beyond the representative. A representative is responsible for payment to Avon on delivery of product to the representative, regardless of whether or not the representative sells the products to end users.

In the traditional direct sales model, a representative contacts customers, selling primarily through the use of brochures that highlight new products and specially priced items for each sales campaign. Sales campaigns generally have a two-week duration in the United States and a three- to four-week duration in most markets outside the United States. Product samples, demonstration products, and selling aids such as make-up color charts are also used. Generally, the representative forwards an order to a designated distribution center. A representative can place an order 24 hours a day, seven days a week using mail, telephone, fax, or the Internet. The order is processed and the products are assembled at the distribution center and delivered to the representative, usually by a local delivery service. The representative then delivers the merchandise and collects payment from the customer.

The recruiting and training of representatives are the primary responsibilities of District Sales Managers. District Sales Managers are employees of

Avon and are paid a salary and a sales incentive based primarily on the increase over the prior year's sales of Avon products by representatives in their district. Personal contacts, including recommendations from current representatives (including the Sales Leadership program), and local advertising constitute the primary means of obtaining new representatives. The Sales Leadership program is a modified network marketing selling system that gives representatives the opportunity to earn commissions on their own sales and bonuses from sales of representatives they have recruited. Development of the Sales Leadership program throughout the world is part of Avon's long-term growth strategy. Because of the high rate of turnover among representatives, a characteristic of direct sales, recruiting and training of new representatives are continually necessary.

## ENTER THE INTERNET: DISINTERMEDIATION OR REINTERMEDIATION?

In 1998, as the Internet began to expand rapidly as a sale channel, Avon management initiated an aggressive business process redesign in an effort to reduce the costs of its entire production, management, and distribution systems, all of which relied on outdated mainframe software programs inherited from the 1960s. Consultants were hired, people who supposedly understood the new Internet business model. Their recommendation was to disintermediate (eliminate) the sales force. Once rid of the expensive, revenue-draining sales force, the new thinking suggested a powerful direct online model through Avon.com and strategic alliances with other Web audience aggregators such as iVillage, WebMD, Amazon, and MSN.com.

Fortunately Avon's management rejected the "new thinking" of the Web-centric model and invented a new model that it called a "representative-centric" Web sales model, which would achieve two goals: strengthen the ability of the sales reps to serve their customers and reduce costs to the company.

The numbers tell the tale. Avon reps fill out paper forms when placing an order that sometimes can reach 50 pages in length. The cost of processing the order—not including the rep's time to generate, track, and store the order—is

$1.50. For orders entered online, the costs drop to 30 cents. With more than a million orders per week, the company generates $478 million in savings and additional annual profits. Although sales reps collect a 40% commission on their sales, they bring new customers to the company virtually for nothing. The customer acquisition cost over the Internet was estimated in 2000 to be at least $35 per customer, and it was much higher in 2003 and is expected to be even higher in 2004 as competitors push Web advertising costs higher. To bring in 10 million new Internet customers—roughly the size of the customer base in Canada—would cost $350 million. Management reasoned that the gains from eliminating the sales force would not cover the customer acquisition costs of the direct Web model.

The direct Web model also had implications for Avon's logistics systems. Its production and shipping systems were set up to process medium-sized orders from sales reps—essentially independent businesses. The systems were not set to handle orders for one or two items. The direct Web model, it was assumed, would produce millions of orders each week from direct customers for relatively tiny shipments. To service this new market would require new production systems and distribution mechanisms. All these expenses added to the cost of the Web-centric model.

Instead, the analysis suggested that Avon adopt multiple avenues of selling its cosmetics to customers. In this hybrid model, Avon's representatives would sell to their customers not only face-to-face but online as well through their own Web sites, called YourAvon.com. Avon would develop a template for traditional reps where they could enter orders and where their customers could order directly from the rep. Avon called these new hybrid online/offline reps "e-representatives." At the same time, Avon itself would sell its products online via www.avon.com to customers who didn't want to buy from Avon ladies—customers Avon.com calls "channel rejecters."

Avon would also pursue other ways to sell more cosmetics, primarily through retail stores and kiosks that would be located at brick-and-mortar malls. The Avon.com team presented the plan to the Avon Board of Directors in September 1999, and the Board signed off on it. One year later, on September 27, 2000, the revamped Avon.com business-to-consumer (B2C) and YourAvon.com business-to-business (B2B) sites went live, as did the company's MyAvon.com online portal for reps, managers, and Avon employees.

# FUTURE PROSPECTS

The various distinctions and terminology used by Avon have proved somewhat confusing. An Avon customer can buy Avon products from either Avon.com or YourAvon.com. Avon reps manage their sales efforts through YourAvon.com but find news about the company and its rep programs through Avon.com. The company still has a long way to go to justify the $60 million or more it said it would spend on the Web over the course of three years, in pursuit of a strategy that—in the words of Avon.com general manager and president Edwards—produced minuscule revenue and profit results for Avon. The company does not report in its Annual Reports the amount of sales by channel. However, industry experts believe that Avon may have reached the $100 million level in annual sales of Avon.com and YourAvon.com combined. If so, these sales would amount to less than 2% of Avon's business.

Right now, in 2004, the company is not pushing reps to sell products online. Instead, it is looking for the biggest impact to come from getting reps to order products online. If the company can get half of its reps to order online, the savings from eliminating the collection of paper order forms across the country could be tens of millions of dollars a year, enough to justify the costs of building the new sales channel.

Revenues at Avon continue to grow at a steady but plodding mid-single-digit rate. Management still believes that the results of the Business Transformation Program begun in May 2001 are having a positive effect: "It is expected that the savings from these initiatives will provide additional financial flexibility to achieve profit targets, while enabling further investment in consumer growth strategies. Management believes that initiatives associated with the 2001 and 2002 changes will help the company achieve its target of a 250 basis-point expansion of its operating margin, as compared to the 2001 level, by the end of 2004" (Avon 10-K, 2002). Wall Street remains unimpressed. The Business Transformation Program caused a charge against earnings in 2002 of over $90 million. Gross margins and net margins improved only slightly during the period 2001–2003 while sales growth remained in the single digits.

## SOURCES

"All Dolled Up." *Barron'sOnline*, January 19, 2004.

Avon Products Inc. Form 10-K for the year ended December 31, 2003, filed with the Securities and Exchange Commission on March 4, 2004.

Avon Products Inc. Form 10-K for the year ended December 31, 2002, filed with the Securities and Exchange Commission on February 26, 2003.

Avon Products Inc. Form 10-Q for the quarterly period ended September 30, 2003, filed with the Securities and Exchange Commission on October 29, 2003.

Beatty, Sally. "Avon Tries Knocking on Dormitory Doors." *Wall Street Journal*, March 28, 2003.

Chang, Leslie. "Avon Plans to Expand Reach in China by Adding 500 Stores." *Wall Street Journal*, October 23, 2003.

Mehra, Devina. "Does Avon Still Look Great?" *Barron's Online*, December 22, 2003.

# Reed Elsevier Internet Marketing Strategy:

## Digital Bundling and the "Big Deal" Drive Net Profits but Rouse Opposition

Reed Elsevier is one of the world's leading publishers and information providers, with revenues of over $6 billion in 2003 and net income of about $300 million. Reed Elsevier's main lines of business are scientific, legal, educational, and business publishing. The company employs 29,000 people worldwide, with principal operations in North America and Europe. Among the information industry brand names owned by Reed Elsevier are Lexis/Nexis (the legal information database), Matthew Bender (legal analysis), Martindale-Hubbell (legal directories), and Butterworth and Tolley (U.K. legal publisher). The company also owns business magazines such as *Variety, Interior Design, Computer Weekly*, and vertical portals such as manufacturing.net, reedtelevision.com, e-insite.com, variety.com, and wirelessweek.com. In 2001, Reed Elsevier bought Harcourt Publishing, and in 2002, it sold off the higher education arm, Harcourt Higher Education, to Thomson, retaining Harcourt's significant collection of science, technology, and medical journals (STM). The combined collection of STM journals makes it the largest in the world.

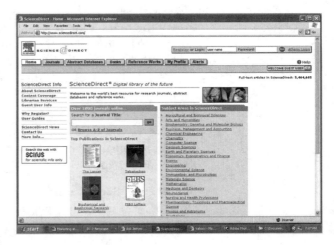

In science publications, Reed Elsevier owns ScienceDirect, the world's largest collection of online digital science, technology, and medical journals. This segment of the company's business provides scientific information to research libraries and scientists through journals, books, CD-ROMs, and a family of Internet-based products, sold under the brand name ScienceDirect.

# SCIENCEDIRECT

The world's first scientific journal was the *Lancet*, first published in 1823 and dedicated to "putting an end to mystery and concealment" in the world of medicine. In 2004, there are an estimated 164,000 scientific journals published worldwide in all disciplines. About 16% of these journals are available online. According to Blackwell's periodical price index, STM journals have risen in price 178% to 184% over the last ten years, with increases averaging 5% to 25% per year, far above rates of inflation in North America and Europe. The size of the market for academic journals in the United States is estimated to be about $20 billion annually. Scientific journals are purchased primarily by university libraries and industrial research laboratories. A subscription to a single print journal costs several thousand dollars per year, and for university libraries, which may subscribe to over 2,000 journals, each read by a few scholars per year, the costs can be extraordinarily high, especially on a per article read basis. For this reason, many smaller universities restrict their subscriptions to a hundred or so journals purchased at the request of academic departments and individual professors.

In 1999, Reed Elsevier launched ScienceDirect as an Internet-based repository of STM journals. Spending slightly over $400 million per year for three years, the company opened a factory in the Philippines, where 2,000 workers scanned back issues of scientific journals. Some 4.5 million journal articles are now online, a number expected to reach 6 million by 2005. In 2003, there were 84 million requests to download articles. The company claims 3,300 ScienceDirect clients and a renewal rate of 96%. Reed has seen its STM revenues double since 1999 to $2.33 billion—about a quarter of all sales and nearly 40% of its operating profit in 2003.

# THE "BIG DEAL"

Reed Elsevier is credited with developing a strategy for coping with the Internet at a time when many other STM publishers were stuck in nineteenth-century journal-publishing practices, refusing to produce digital versions of their journals for fear they would lose control over copyrighted information. Reed Elsevier's strategy was to spend a very substantial amount of money to digitize its holdings of scientific journals, purchase other firms' STM content or the entire company (such as Harcourt) to increase the attractiveness of its holdings and fend off competition, and then to offer customers a bundle of digital journals rather than encouraging the purchase of just a few journals. Once it had scanned a large part of its company-owned STM journals, it approached libraries and research labs with a bundle of over 1,500 online digital journals priced at a substantial markup from the library's current expenditures for a smaller number of journals (usually several hundred) but at a substantial discount on a per journal basis. Hence libraries were offered access to a vast library of journals that in the past they could not afford.

Thousands of universities worldwide bought the package. The library at Drexel University in Philadelphia, for instance, subscribed to fewer than 100 print journals from Reed Elsevier because of the high cost of several thousand dollars per journal. Now that it has joined ScienceDirect, Drexel's library has online access to over 1,500 journals in the Reed Elsevier database at a substantial increase in cost for the bundle but a decrease in cost per journal to a few hundred dollars.

## OPPOSITION TO THE BIG DEAL THREATENS REED ELSEVIER'S BRAND IMAGE

Universities typically sign multi-year contracts with ScienceDirect for electronic access to the large library of journals. When universities resist paying the high price for the bundle and seek instead to "unbundle" the offering and choose a smaller number of journals, they find that Reed's inflexible pricing schedules forces them to give up a large number of journals before they start saving any money. In addition, there are few, if any, competitors to Reed's service and even if there were, universities would experience high switching costs in moving to other services. As a result, Reed has been able to push through price increases of 7% a year during the last two years.

But the Web cuts both ways insofar as it increases transparency (i.e., the ease with which consumers can find out actual prices and costs in a marketplace). Cornell University, an Ivy League school, was paying ScienceDirect $1.7 million a year for access to 930 journals. In fact, the Reed Elsevier journals accounted for 20% of Cornell's total periodicals budget. But unlike printed journals, Cornell librarians could use their campus intranet servers to see exactly how many students and professors were actually accessing these journals. Librarians discovered that hundreds of the journals it purchased in the bundle were never read, and several hundred more were read very infrequently. As a result, Cornell is now negotiating with Reed Elsevier to eliminate 150 journals and substantially reduce its annual subscription costs for Reed Elsevier journals. The Faculty Senate at Cornell University adopted a strongly worded resolution supporting its library in canceling hundreds of Elsevier journals. The resolution read in part: "Recognizing that the cost of Elsevier journals in particular is radically out of proportion with the importance of those journals to the library's serials collection (measured both in terms of the proportion of the total collection they represent and in terms of their use by and value to faculty and students), the University Faculty Senate encourages the library to seek in the near term, in consultation with the faculty, to reduce its expenditures on Elsevier journals to no more than 15% of its total annual serials acquisitions expenditures (from in excess of 20% in 2003)." Harvard is following suit, seeking to reduce its ScienceDirect journals by 100 titles to save several hundred thousand dollars per year.

Critics argue that the "big deal" in effect requires libraries to take more journals than they might otherwise choose from commercial publishers such as Reed Elsevier. The limits on the libraries' abilities to change the package in the "big deal" result in cuts in subscriptions to journals from other publishers whenever the libraries face financial constraints. A further implication of these arrangements is that citations to the commercial publishers' journals are likely to increase at the expense of the not-for-profit sector, thus increasing the apparent value of those journals.

# EMERGING OPEN ACCESS MOVEMENT

Although Reed Elsevier was an Internet pioneer in bringing STM journals to online environments and in broadening considerably the number of journals accessible in many universities, the company is now being perceived widely by critics as exploiting a near-monopoly position with pricing policies that are felt to be unfair.

Efforts to make the results of publicly funded science free and open to everyone are not new. As early as 1991, the physicist Paul Ginsparg established an Internet server, arxiv.org, to which physicists could post digital copies of their manuscripts prior to publication. This server expanded from its initial role as a vehicle for sharing preprints in theoretical high-energy physics to its current role as the principal "library" for a large fraction of research literature in physics, computer sciences, astronomy, and many mathematical specialties. Today, more than half of all research articles in physics are posted to this server prior to their publication in conventional journals. In many fields, these "e-prints" are the de facto publications of record. In 1999, Nobel prize winner Dr. Harold Varmus, then-director of the National Institutes of Health (NIH), presented an ambitious proposal for NIH to develop and operate an electronic publishing site that would provide barrier-free access to the peer-reviewed and pre-peer-reviewed life sciences literature. The plan evolved considerably in a year of vigorous public discussion. The result, PubMed Central (PMC), was launched in February 2000 with content from the *Proceedings of the National Academy of Sciences* and *Molecular Biology of the Cell*. To allay publishers' concerns about lost revenues, participating publishers were not required to deposit material immediately on publication, and most opted for a delay of between six months and a year. Despite these allowances, few journals followed PNAS and MBC in joining PMC. Many publishers expressed opposition to the venture, and lobbying efforts in Congress were successful in having PMC funding cut off.

In October 2000, a coalition of research scientists founded the Public Library of Science (PLOS). PLOS is dedicated to making the world's scientific and medical literature a public resource. PLOS's first action was to circulate an open letter calling on scientific publishers to make archival scientific research literature available for distribution through free online public libraries of science such as PubMed Central. The open letter was signed by over 30,000 scientists from 180 countries. This initiative prompted some significant and welcome steps by many scientific publishers toward freer access to published research, but in general STM publishers such as Reed Elsevier have failed to respond. Currently PLOS publishes the first peer-reviewed open access journal in biology (called *PLOS Biology*).

## REED ELSEVIER'S MARKETING CHALLENGE

Reed Elsevier management currently denies that there is a problem with ScienceDirect pricing policies and does not envisage making any changes in its marketing strategy. Mark Armour, Reed Elsevier's finance director, dismissed talk of new threats to its science journal model as a "lot of noise." However, Wall Street analysts are concerned about the threat that free online scientific research could pose to Reed Elsevier's pricing power as ScienceDirect contracts come up for renewal. While Reed Elsevier's share price outperformed other media companies in 2002, in 2003 the shares fell 12%.

Now bigger players are getting into the game that could give more power to the Internet open access model. A bill (the Public Access to Science Act ) introduced in the United States Congress by Representative Martin Olav Sabo (D-Minn) in June 2003, would remove copyright protection for all publicly funded research and require it to be placed in the public domain. In December 2003, the British House of Commons Science and Technology Committee opened an inquiry into the scientific publications industry.

With clouds gathering, Reed Elsevier management may try to weather the storm in order to sustain its high margins on scientific publications. Alternatively, it may be forced to develop a new marketing strategy for ScienceDirect that does not alienate either its scientific authors or its library customers.

## SOURCES

"Economic Analysis of Scientific Research Publishing." *Wellcome Trust*, January 2003.

Goldsmith, Charles. "Net Profits: Reed Elsevier Had a Clear Internet Strategy and It Stuck to It." *Wall Street Journal*, September 22, 2003.

Goldsmith, Charles. "Reed Elsevier Feels Resistance to Web Pricing." *Wall Street Journal*, January 19, 2004.

U.S. Census Bureau. Statistical Abstract of the United States 2002 Table No. 1097: "Information Sector Services—Estimated Revenue: 1998 to 2000." 2003.

U.S. House of Representatives. 108th Congress, H.R. 2613, The Public Access to Science Act, June 23, 2003.

Wary, Richard. "Reed Elsevier at Risk as MPs Look Into Science Publishing Market." *The Guardian*, December 12, 2003.

# Advergames:

## "Engage Your Customer, Get Personal, Make a Sale, Have Fun"

Think you can score against a National Hockey League goalie? Want to find out? If you go to www.nhl.com/nextel you can play a game in which you get the chance to score against an NHL goalie. You will have to register, of course, and answer some questions about yourself (such as "Will you be purchasing a cell phone in the next week, month, or year?"). The sponsor of the game is Nextel, one of the fastest-growing cell phone companies in the United States. But once you've registered, you get to play the game and take your swipes at the goalie. Nextel hopes that you'll tell your friends about this exciting game and they will join the fun. Think viral marketing: soon Nextel will have millions of people playing the game. When you tire of that game, move on over to BMW's USA site (http://www.bmwusa.com) and play the X3 Adventure online game. You can take on killer moguls, take a jarring ride down a mountain, or splash in the frothy water of a kayaking run with a new simulated BMW X3 SUV. If this is a bit much, then you might want to try a more leisurely game. Go to www.adveract.com and try out Wordsense, a game created by a marketing firm in which you build words off of other words from a limited pool of letters. You have to play fast because the letters disappear, and depending on your skill, you could make the worldwide "leader board," where the scores of top players are displayed. There are three different game modes, Speed Challenge, Infinite, and Round-Based, that each require unique strategies. A new batch of games is available every day and as you play, you can enjoy the ragtime sound track, or listen to your own MP3s with the game's MP3 player. But be aware: this game's for hire. Advertisers can license the game software and insert their product brand names into the game at strategic moments of play.

These are just three of the hundreds of online games you can find being used to create interactive advertising environments. "Advergames" are highly interactive advertisements put into the form of a multimedia game. Among the major companies worldwide using this form of advertising include Mercedes Benz, Tommy Hilfiger, Pepsi, Microsoft, and Coors.

In the next three years we can expect to see double-digit growth in advergames. The reason is quite simple: this is where the eyeballs will increasingly turn in the United States and Europe. The era of 30-second spot TV commercials capturing significant parts of the 18-to-34 year-old market are nearing an end. There is a battle raging for media mindshare, and traditional advertising venues—newspapers, magazines, broadcast television—are losing. In 1965, 80% of the 18-to-49 year-olds in the United States could be reached with three 60-second TV spots. In 2004, it would take 117 60-second spots to produce the same result. Viewers are moving to video games (both online and on consoles), "on demand" cable television services (paid movies) without advertising, and the Internet itself for entertainment. The large mass audience of the past is fragmenting into many smaller audiences found in front of game consoles or at a variety of different Internet sites and sometimes playing games or other interactive activities. To make matters worse for traditional advertising venues, technologies such as digital video and Tivo recorders are making it possible for viewers to zap commercials completely from recorded television shows.

For advertisers, the solution to the problems of audience fragmentation and competing media such as the Internet and games is straightforward: put the advertising where the eyeballs are.

Worldwide video game software sales totalled near $24 billion in 2003, and spending will grow faster over the next four years than in any other entertainment and media market, according to PricewaterhouseCoopers. Electronic Arts, the leading video game maker, is now the fourth largest software company in the world, behind Microsoft, Oracle, and SAP. The average American will spend 75 hours in 2003 playing video games, double the amount of time spent in 1997, and only Internet usage is growing faster, according to the market research firm Veronis Suhler Stevenson. The growing adoption of broadband Internet, the popularity of console gaming, and the emergence of "next generation" mobile technologies are driving the video game market to new levels. Video gaming has not quite penetrated all demographics segments yet, but the day is not far away. The "battle for mainstream" is on.

Online games, whether board, card, or trivia games, are popular among all demographic segments, and it is not surprising that the "big three" portals, Yahoo!, MSN, and AOL, have created some of the most popular game sites (Figure 4-1). Data from Nielsen/NetRatings show that 16.5 million U.S. Internet users visited gaming sites in one week ending August 17, 2003, with Yahoo! Games attracting the largest audience.

**Figure 4-1    Top Ten Gaming Sites Among At-Home Internet Users in the United States in the Week Ending August 17, 2003 (unique audience, in thousands)**

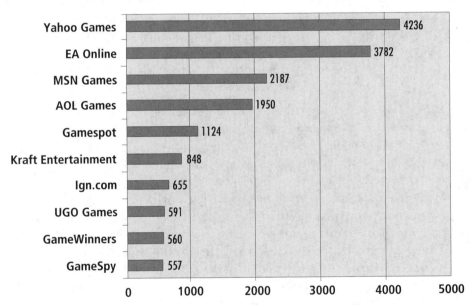

Source: Nielsen/Net Ratings, August 2003, reported in "Console Wars II: The Battle for Mainstream," eMarketer, January 2004.

Advergames—a mix of advertising and games—are not new. The first examples appeared in 1999, but the technology for online gaming was so poor that they did not attract a large following. With the widespread distribution of Macromedia's Flash and Shockwave and the growth of high-speed broadband Internet connections, however, the new online games are starting to live up to their promise. The promise is to create an intimate, online, engaging relationship with the consumer that can be used over time to sell products. According to a recent survey by Gartner, over 40% of the U.S. online population played at least one game online in 2003.

Advergames fall into the category of marketing called *relationship marketing*, where the object is to build a relationship based on knowledge of the consumer's personal preferences. In *awareness marketing*—such as banner ads—consumers have a fleeting relationship with the product (similar to a 30-second TV commercial). They are exposed to a picture with some text, and then the message is clicked away. In *transactional marketing*, consumers are encouraged to buy, usually right now, and the relationship lasts about as long as it takes to complete the transaction. Price and availability tend to be the main drivers for transactional marketing. In *consultatitive marketing*, consumers are exposed to information on how to use the product. The relationship lasts longer than with other forms and provides opportunities for advertisers to learn more about their customers. In *relationship marketing*, the idea is to engage the consumer for a long enough period of time to gather real insight into his or her preferences, values, styles, likes, and dislikes.

Here's how it works. First, to play a game, users have to register. Usually the registration is quick and uncomplicated (name and e-mail address), but many firms also collect data about preferences, occupation, age, and future purchasing intentions at this point as well. There's usually a prechecked box that says, "Would you like to receive more information by e-mail about this product?" Most consumers leave this box clicked, which permits the advertiser to create an "opt in" e-mail marketing list. The gathering of background information on the user begins the building of a customer profile record. During the game, additional information can be gathered to fill out the customer profile record. For instance, in the middle of the game, a sweepstakes announcement may pop up offering the consumer a chance to win a large sum of money by entering more personal information. After passing this point, the consumer may be offered a chance to compete against others in a global game competition in return for entering additional information. At the end of the game, the consumer will be asked to recommend the game to another user. One potential of advergames is that they can have a viral quality: the word on where to find really good, fun games can quickly spread among friends who share an interest.

Many of these features of advergames are demonstrated in what is, arguably, one of the most wildly popular advergames for 2003–2004. U.K. soft drinks company Britvic asked Graphico, a U.K. marketing firm, to create a viral campaign for its fruit juice drink, J$_2$O, to increase brand awareness of J$_2$O as an alternative to alcohol among young men and women, ages 18–35. In response, Graphico developed an advergame called the Toilet Training game. As users consume virtual alcohol, they must pay a visit to the toilet and are then challenged to keep their aim on the toilet bowl. Points are gained for keeping the stream in the toilet. The game makes accuracy progressively harder, but

drinking a virtual bottle of J$_2$O gives users another chance to stay in the game. Players can register their score for the chance to win a night on the town with four friends and spending money.

Since it was released to consumers on February 11, 2003, the game has had over 2.3 million visitors and over 100,000 opt-in names were captured in just twelve weeks. Katie Rawll, J$_2$O brand controller at Britvic said, "We knew that a viral campaign was a great way to reach our target audience and raise awareness of the J$_2$O brand. Graphico's idea for the J$_2$O e-game was both edgy and slick, and it builds on the existing creative theme. It's exceeded all expectations as over 15,000 people forwarded the game in the first 48 hours after it went live—that's before we even kicked off the campaign on 26 February."

Other companies have experienced similar positive results from advergames. Procter & Gamble, for example, reported a very positive response to its Mission Refresh, an online game in which players help Captain Cool eradicate dandruff creatures using bubbles created by P&G's Head & Shoulders shampoo. Toyota experienced success with its Toyota Adrenaline racing game. Research found that the game attracted frequent repeat players who spent about 20 minutes each time with the game, far longer than a consumer spends with a typical advertisement on the Internet. It also significantly enhanced brand awareness of Toyota among users, raising it from sixth among major car companies to second, according to Wild Tangent, developer of the Toyota game, as well as a similar game for Radio Shack. In the Radio Shack game, players select a replica of one of the dozens of remote controlled cars sold by Radio Shack, and drive it around a virtual 3-D Radio Shack store, exposing them to other Radio Shack merchandise as they play.

But designing successful advergames is an art and fraught with potential dangers. Just sticking product into a game and hoping users will visit your Web site is not a good approach. People may play the game but never engage the product or remember your firm. Advergames seem to work best for new products—such as $J_2O$—when they create a memorable experience the users would like to share with others. With more established products, such as BMW cars, successful advergames put the product into the action and build the game around the product so that the user can actually experience the product. In the BMW game described earlier, the consumer customizes the colors on the BMW game car and "drives" the new model X3 in the game.

According to industry experts, advergames alone are not sufficient to market a product. Rather, advergames should be seen as one part of an integrated campaign that includes advertising in traditional media, online sweepstakes and contests, and traditional banner ads.

With these cautions in mind, the role of advergames in marketing is likely to increase. There are several drivers. Consumers are tiring of traditional ad formats and are increasingly attracted to rich media formats. The software art of game design has also advanced along with advances in computer processor power and bandwidth. Perhaps most important, advergames are exceptionally successful in gathering data for consumer profiles voluntarily from game players who seem willing to give up significant information about themselves in order to play the game. As a result, advertisers using games have found that advergames—when compared to other more fleeting advertising methods—result in much higher brand awareness, customer loyalty, product and feature awareness, site traffic, and time spent on site.

# SOURCES

Bryan, Nancy Wong. "More and More Marketers Got Game." iMedia.com, January 26, 2004.

Eng, Paul. "Playing the Ad Game. Marketers Use Online Games to Make Soft Sales Pitches." ABC News, November 12, 2003.

"Far Beyond Branding, How Nextel Collects Invaluable Data from Sports Advergames Players," *Marketing Sherpa*, August 4, 2003.

"J$_2$O." Graphico New Media, February 18, 2004.

"The Future of Advergames," www.watercoolergames.org, February 2004.

Peers, Martin. "Buddy, Can You Spare Some Time?" *Wall Street Journal*, January 26, 2004.

# Internet Advertising Movies:

## We Interrupt This E-mail to Bring You an Important Video from Your Sponsor

I s your Internet experience turning more and more into a TV-like experience? If you're like most Web users these days, you don't spend endless hours surfing the Web aimlessly but instead seek out targeted searches, specific URLs, and products you already know you want. But just like television, where you don't control the ad stream, you are bombarded by ads you don't want to see, pop-up ads that seem to come from nowhere (at least no place you clicked), ads that hang around when you close a page or sometimes pop up when you go to a page, or sometimes pop up right in the middle of the

page you want to look at (like the *New York Times* front page). This is not "personalization" but its opposite, de-personalization.

The increasingly large-sized ads that flash in separate windows above or below Web pages are among the most annoying and objectionable aspects of using the Internet. Unfortunately, pop-up ads are profitable for advertisers and are a major source of revenue for Internet publishers. Pop-ups capture users attention and get them to focus on the product. Static banner ads still make up a sizable but declining portion of Web advertising, but they are not as effective as pop-ups, and because of this, they are much less profitable. Figure 5-1 identifies the top five pop-up and pop-under advertisers as of December 2003 (pop-unders are the ads that appear when you leave a site).

**Figure 5-1   Top Five Pop-up and Pop-under Advertisers as of December 2003**

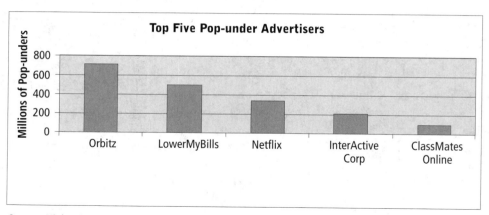

Source: Nielsen/NetRatings, AdRelevance, reported in Hansell (2004).

Pop-ups have become so irritating to millions of Web users that Yahoo!, AOL, Microsoft, and Google now distribute software that allows users to block pop-ups, and big Internet service providers such as EarthLink are distributing similar software to their users. Microsoft plans to add a pop-up blocker to its Windows XP upgrade. It's ironic that the very companies making money off the pop-ups—portals—are the ones that are distributing the blocking software. The reason is a flood of e-mail and complaints from users.

The growing consumer resistance to intrusive pop-ups has had an impact. In December 2001, 1.4% of the Web ads were pop-ups or pop-unders, as measured by Nielsen/NetRatings. The percentage rose to 8.7% in July 2003 but declined in December 2003 to 6.3%. Advertising firms that rely on pop-ups are experiencing a rude awakening: today, 20% to 25% of Web users have pop-up blocking enabled on their computers, more than double the number in 2003. Both Google and Yahoo have added a pop-up blocker to the toolbars they offer free of charge to users. And Microsoft's MSN just added a pop-up blocker to its most recent software. The revolt of consumers against pop-ups and spam e-mail is forcing firms to spend more advertising dollars on traditional media and direct marketing (Hansell, 2004).

While smaller Web publishers still remain dependent on pop-up revenues, larger Web publishers are attempting to reduce their reliance on pop-ups. For instance, today, pop-ups account for less than 1% of Sportsline's advertising revenue, down from 5% to 10% a few years ago. Mark J. Mariani, Sporstline president of sales and marketing, claims "We are totally ready for the day when you can't have any pop-ups. Clients have started to shy away from pop-ups and pop-unders." Sportsline now employs a quota system so that only one pop-up ad will be shown to a user in any 12-hour period. In order to compensate for losses in revenue, Sportsline and many other publishers are emphasizing larger-sized advertisements that can be placed within the pages of their main sites.

"There is a consumer revolt as forms of advertising get more intrusive," said Rob Kaiser, vice president for narrowband marketing at EarthLink. EarthLink was the first large Internet service provider to develop and advertise pop-up blocking to its installed base of Internet consumers. Over 1 million of Earthlink's 5 million customers have installed Earthlink's pop-up blocking software since 2002, when Earthlink first offered it.

Advertising executives in both the television and the Internet markets protest that consumers who block the ads are undercutting the economic model that provides them with free entertainment and information. Tivo, the popular home TV digital recorder, permits viewers to systematically block commercials. David Moore, CEO of 24/7 Real Media, an Internet advertising firm, admits that "I haven't spoken to any people who say I love pop-ups, send me more of them, but they are part of a quid pro quo. If you want to enjoy the content of a Web site that is free, the pop-ups come with it" (Hansell, 2004).

As might be expected, advertising networks that serve up an estimated 1 billion pop-up ads a month are still supporting the format. For instance, the Internet ad network operated by DoubleClick is developing technology that will enable pop-up ads to evade the blocking software no matter what the individual consumer wants. "There are advertisers who want pop-up ads and publishers that want to serve them," said Douglas Knopper, general manager for online advertising at DoubleClick. "Our role is to help them do that" (Hansell, 2004).

# STREAMING VIDEO ADS

But while the boom in pop-ups has definitely popped, there's a whole new generation of high-motion, agitated advertising about to come your way: video commercials (or just plain old TV commercials) will be moving into Instant Messages, e-mail, and other popular Web pages in the coming years. And you thought the Internet was different from TV? Think again.

It started in May 2003 with ESPN's Motion service, which used Disney proprietary software to stream high-quality 30-frame-per-second interviews and announcements, along with advertising, to users with broadband connections. This experiment was so successful that an entire new industry of Internet video streaming sprang up to service advertisers hungry for new ways to contact the Internet audience that is slowly slipping away from the grasp of network television ads. Of course what was different about ESPN Motion is that users voluntarily signed up for the service. In January 2004, more than a dozen Web sites, including MSN, ESPN, Lycos, and iVillage, began serving up the first full-motion online video commercials—from Pepsi, AT&T, Honda, Vonage, and Warner Brothers—in a six-week test. "It's TV without the television," said John Vail, director of digital media and marketing for Pepsi-Cola North America, a unit of PepsiCo (Tedeschi, 2004).

The new video ads differ from previous Internet video ads because they play at TV video quality of 30 frames a second. The older multimedia ads were much less sharp than TV images, even for people with fast connections, and could play only in a tiny window. The new video ads are much larger and can even go full screen without the user clicking anything.

The leading advertising technology companies involved are Unicast, EyeWonder, and EyeBlaster. The new ad technology from Unicast, for instance, loads the commercial in the background while users view a Web page. Then, when the user clicks on a new page, the full-motion ad displays full screen. Even with a low-speed connection, the new advertising technology can display an advertisement that looks remarkably similar to a television ad. And what happens to user control? Users can click a box to stop the ad and proceed with their browsing. Unicast claims the ads do not really interfere with the user's browser because the actual loading takes place in the background when the user is inactive.

During the six-week test, between January 20 and February 29, 2004, Unicast served 100 million ads. Pepsi reused two advertising segments it created for television. In one, titled "Just Lunch," a dog steals its owner's sandwich and Pepsi, and replaces them with a cat. In the other, "Vacuum," a vacuum cleaner hunts a Pepsi drinker and eats his pants. Following exposure to the full-motion ads, users were given opportunities to follow links to traditional Pepsi ads on the Pepsi Web site. However, Pepsi remains undecided about the future use of these ads. A Pepsi spokesman said that although some might feel the ads were intrusive, they were nevertheless far more entertaining and of higher quality than anything users had seen before on the Web (Tedeschi, 2004).

Research firms such as Forrester expect demand for these new kinds of ads to mushroom due to their novelty and the fact that they offer a much more engaging viewing experience for consumers. Forrester believes they will be viewed in a more favorable light by consumers than pop-ups because the ads do not slow user browsing and are under partial user control. Growth in the use of the ads will be further enhanced by the fact that they play using Windows Media Player, which 8 out of 10 Web surfers already have installed.

Another factor in the future growth of full motion advertising is the widespread adoption of high-speed Internet connections. Richard V. Hopple, Unicast's chief executive officer, said his firm is releasing Unicast's "video commercial" technology now because high-speed broadband connections now reach 49.5 million homes (about 38% of all households), according to Nielsen/NetRatings, an Internet research firm. In addition, 50 million people surf the Web at work and about 94% of these at-work surfers have broadband connections, according to comScore Networks, another Internet research firm (Tedeschi, 2004).

But Forrester and other analysts are worried that, given the online advertising industries' past history, it will be unable to exercise self-restraint. With the growth in mobile high speed connections, Wi-Fi, and 3G telephone services, and the continued rapid growth in home and business broadband, Internet publishers will be strongly attracted to any advertising technology than can grab the viewer's attention.

The commercial appeal of these new ads for advertisers is reflected in their higher prices. Publishers such as Disney's ESPN.com plan to charge as much as $35 for every thousand ads displayed, about twice as much as large television networks charge for prime time television. If so, this means that Internet full-motion advertising for the first time in history is being valued higher than television spot ads. However, there is some reason to believe that an online video ad is, in fact, worth more than a television spot commercial. Researchers at the London School of Economics have found that television viewers will do nearly anything to avoid a commercial, and when in groups, people will ignore the commercial completely and (horrors!) talk to each other. The Internet viewer, according to the study, is a "lonely but far more attentive viewer." Hence, Internet viewers might be more affected by an online ad.

As noted previously, ESPN was among the first to use TV-quality video ads online with its Motion service, initially introduced in May 2003. ESPN's Motion service allows users to download software that permits them to play full-motion highlights from sporting events. Between the sporting event programs, users are shown 15- or 30-second full-motion ads that play at 30 frames per second. However, while the Unicast display is full-screen, the ESPN Motion service plays in only half a screen, and the ad cannot be turned off. ESPN claims that 2.5 million users have downloaded the free software, and that about 700,000 users view sports video and ad clips every day. The list of companies trying the new service includes Lexus, McDonald's, and IBM. ESPN says that the service has created more demand than they can satisfy. According to Unicast, one of the reasons for this success is that the advertiser can surround the consumer nearly 24/7. During the day, branding messages are delivered on the Internet, and during the evening the same message is delivered on television. It's like "surround advertising."

Consumer reaction to the new ads thus far has been one of heightened awareness, novelty and even excitement. Some publishers believe, at least for now, that if the advertising is done well, it's just as good as the entertainment or show. However, MSN's Joanne Bradford, a vice president and the chief media revenue officer for Microsoft's MSN, says that MSN will not show more than one video commercial per user in a 24 hour period. If users complain, they will stop the format entirely. But so far, MSN viewers have not complained. Other online publishers are taking a wait and see approach. CBS Marketwatch, a financial news site, has declined to join the full-motion ad movement. Executives at CBS Marketwatch are fearful of alienating users, and disturbing work environments. Because so much of Web use for this site occurs at work, a more subtle sound experience is required.

Online publishers are excited about the full-motion ads as a new source of ad revenue, which plunged after the e-commerce bubble burst in 2001. In 2002, Internet ads were difficult to give away, and many professionals believed Internet advertising would never command the attention of major brand marketers such as automobile companies, or consumer products companies such as Proctor & Gamble. But officials at firms such as Honda are looking for the new ads to improve their online effectiveness. Honda ad executives say that the problem with TV ads is that they never know how many people actually see the ad. But with Internet advertising, Honda can determine precisely how many people saw the ad, and also track the user to find out what they did after they saw the ad. Potentially there is far more value in Internet advertising (Tedeschi, 2004).

The move toward full-motion video ads on the Internet is being driven by a number of forces. First there has been a huge turnaround in general Internet advertising, which sagged after the Internet bubble burst in 2000. Online ad revenues have posted five quarters of steady growth since the beginning of 2002, with advertising up 35% in 2003 compared to 2002 at large Web sites such as Yahoo! and MSN. While much of this growth is due to retailers and financial services and travel services—mainstays of the Internet ad mix—in 2003 and 2004, the consumer products companies, such as Unilever, Gillette, and Procter & Gamble, joined the rush to online advertising. The rapid growth in broadband access is another factor in the growth of online video ads, as is the growth in Flash animation advertising. And advertising technology companies are finally producing products that allow 30-frames-per-second quality ads to play without the user's surfing being interrupted. EyeWonder, for instance, makes a boxed software tool called Studio G3 that allows ad agencies to create their own streaming videos easily.

But another reason we are likely to experience a rapid growth in online video ads is simply that they are more effective than banners or pop-ups. In one government experience, the U.S. Department of Homeland Security compared rich media public service ads (PSAs) to other forms such as pop-ups and banners. The governmental office, in partnership with the Advertising Council, examined the effectiveness of the online component of the Homeland Security public service advertising "Ready" campaign. The study found that online video ads, streaming via technology from EyeWonder, Inc., significantly increased awareness of the campaign-directed Web-site www.ready.gov. In addition, Web surfers who were exposed to the ads were more likely than others to say that they intended to visit Ready.gov. EyeWonder's streaming Web ads, featuring New York City first responders as well as the U.S. Department of Homeland Security Secretary Tom Ridge, were a significant component of a national cross-media campaign developed in partnership with the Ad Council (Anfuso, 2003).

People exposed to the Web ads on the site were significantly more likely to say that they were likely to visit ready.gov. Among all segments, the Web ads delivered a "lift" of approximately 4% in terms of Web users' intent to visit. The Web ads significantly drove up unaided and aided awareness of ready.gov among a key audience segment, middle-income households. Web visitors with repeated exposures (6 + ) to the Web ads were more likely than others to report that they had recently searched for information related to the Web-site (Anfuso, 2003).

Although advertisers are rushing to try out the new format, many are wary that overexposure will kill the golden goose. On national broadcasting and cable networks there are industry standards for how frequently a television show can be interrupted by advertising. Obviously people watch television not to see the ads but to see the show. On the Internet, there are no such standards limiting pop-ups or any other kind of advertising. It all depends on how much consumers at a site will tolerate. Once again, while the hardware, software, and ISP companies who profit from any use of the Internet are initially supporting the growth of online video advertising, they may easily change their minds if consumers start complaining loudly.

Industry self-restraint is one potential answer, even though it has not worked in the past. For instance, America Online launched a new full motion ad service in November 2003 on its AOL Instant Messenger service (Mack, 2003). The new service allows marketers to deliver television-like full motion and full sound commercials in place of a 120- by 60-pixel banner ad at the top of AIM's "Buddy List. New Line Cinema was one of eight charter advertisers who took part in the AOL pilot program. New Line used a trailer to promote *Elf*, a comedy starring Will Ferrell. In order to keep the ads from annoying its AIM audience, AOL limited individual exposure to two ads per 24 hour period, and it did not allow the same ad to be shown twice in a day. AOL also encouraged advertisers to be as creative as possible with the videos, in an effort to make them more acceptable to the AIM user base.

But if industry self-regulation fails, software makers may well have to extend the functionality of their pop-up ad blockers to include pop-up videos. Most people do not want to have their e-mail or Web surfing interrupted with videos they did not request, and consumers may not, in fact, appreciate the "surround advertising" that online advertising firms and Web publishers want to offer.

## SOURCES

Anfuso, Dawn. "EyeWonder PSA Outperforms Other Ads." *iMediaConnection*, November 13, 2003.

Hansell, Saul. "As Consumers Revolt, a Rush to Block Pop-Up Online Ads." *New York Times*, January 19, 2004.

Mack, Ann. "AOL Instant Messenger to run TV-like Ads." *AdWeek*, October 7, 2003.

Murray, Anna. "Johnson and Johnson Tests Moving TV Ads Online." *Marketing Sherpa*, January 6, 2004.

Tedeschi, Bob. "Online Advertising Is Showing Signs of Revival, with Multimedia Playing an Important Role." *New York Times*, May 5, 2003.

Tedeschi, Bob. "Your Web Surfing Is Being Interrupted to Bring You a Paid Video Commercial. Advertisers Think You Will Stick Around." *New York Times*, January 19, 2004.

# E-COMMERCE IN ACTION

# RedEnvelope:

## Unique Gifts in Short Supply

RedEnvelope is an online retailer of upscale gifts. RedEnvelope's goal is to make gift giving—no matter what the occasion or circumstance—easy and fun. RedEnvelope offers an extensive collection of imaginative, original gifts for every occasion, recipient, and budget. The company attempts to maintain superior customer service and gift delivery services in an effort to provide customers with the best possible gift-giving experience and to encourage repeat business. By 2003, RedEnvelope had developed an internal database of over 1.4 million customer names, with approximately 450,000 new customers added in the twelve months ended June 29, 2003. In fiscal 2003, approximately 70% of customer orders were placed through the company Web site, www.redenvelope.com, and the remainder were placed by telephone. On the Web site, the company offers a wide assortment of products in 14 categories, ranging from baby gifts, jewelry, and men's accessories to home and garden gifts. Lower-priced items are in the $20 to $50 price range and are intended for broader consumer appeal. Higher-priced items have more targeted appeal. The Web site features approximately 550 products, increasing to approximately 750 products during the holiday shopping season.

The company also publishes a full-color catalog several times during the year. The catalog generally features approximately 135 products, increasing to approximately 250 products during the holiday shopping season, and it serves as the primary advertising vehicle for the company's Internet operations.

During fiscal 2003, the company mailed 18.7 million catalogs to over 8 million people.

RedEnvelope had $70 million in sales for 2003 and showed revenue growth of 25% over 2002. The company is located in San Francisco and employs 107 people. In November 2003, the company completed an initial public offering, a rare event for a "dot com" company after the plunge in dot com values since January 2000. The stock was offered at $14 and has been selling for around $15 since the IPO.

## THE VISION

RedEnvelope got its start in 1997 as GiftWorksOnline.com. In 1999 it adopted its current name and signature red gift wrapping. The vision of RedEnvelope was to do more than just be another gift site on the Web—instead, it hopes to offer consumers a unique gift-giving "shopping experience." About 50% of online shoppers do not find what they want, according to the Internet consulting firm Creative Good (Schatz, 2003). RedEnvelope and its largest competitors, FindGift.com and 1StopGiftShops.com, are trying to change that. There are four elements to RedEnvelope's unique gift-giving experience: a unique organization of gifts on its home page, proprietary products, high-quality presentation through superior site design and product packaging, and convenience. By selling gifts for almost all occasions and people in one place, RedEnvelope seeks to make the gift-buying process easier for the giver. By organizing products on its Web site by occasion, recipient, life-style, and shops (or themes), customers can reduce the mental confusion they typically face when buying gifts. Customers can register for a gift reminder service, sign up to receive e-mail promotions, view their order history, and request a catalog. To further differentiate its service, many of the products sold by RedEnvelope are either proprietary or developed specifically for RedEnvelope. Some examples of products available only at RedEnvelope include a four-leaf clover pressed in glass ($28); a range of Kama Sutra kits, with edible items such as honey dust and Love Liquid ($25); and a branding iron for monogramming barbecued steaks ($65) (Barker, 2003).

Finally, to differentiate the experience of receiving RedEnvelope gifts, RedEnvelope delivers gift-wrapped products to the recipient in its trademark high-quality red box with a hand-tied ivory ribbon.

## BUSINESS MODEL

RedEnvelope markets products through its Web site and catalogs. At the time an order is taken, the customer's credit card information is taken, and when the order is shipped, the customer's credit card is charged. The company's revenues consist of product sales, shipping revenue, and gift-wrapping revenue. In the past, the shipping revenue was based on the order value and the method of delivery. As the order value increased, the delivery charge increased as well. After August 25, 2003, the company changed the delivery charge for standard ground delivery to a flat rate regardless of the order value. Gift-wrapping revenue consists of amounts the company charges for its signature red gift boxes. The customer has the option of purchasing gift wrap if the product is offered with special gift wrapping. The gift-wrapping process occurs as part of order fulfillment at the distribution center. No single customer accounts for more than 1% of net revenues. Historically, revenues have been seasonal. Revenues have been higher in the third fiscal quarter, reflecting higher consumer holiday spending.

## FINANCIAL ANALYSIS

In fiscal 2003, RedEnvelope's revenues were $70 million, small by retail standards for national firms, but impressively higher than revenues five years earlier in 1999 of only $1.7 million. By any measure, RedEnvelope has shown extraordinary net revenue growth. Likewise RedEnvelope has demonstrated rapid growth in gross margins to 48% in 2003, which is more typical of retail stores, made possible by a declining cost of sales due to marketing and branding efforts by the firm (Table 6-1).

| Table 6-1 | RedEnvelope Statements of Operations and Summary Balance Sheet Data, 1999–2003 |
|---|---|

**Statements of Operations** (in thousands)

| For the fiscal year ended March 30 | 2003 | 2002 | 2001 | 2000 | 1999 |
|---|---|---|---|---|---|
| Net revenues | 70,059 | 55,778 | 32,565 | 8,035 | 1,764 |
| Cost of sales | 36,577 | 31,446 | 19,800 | 5,899 | 1,257 |
| **Gross profit** | 33,482 | 24,332 | 12,765 | 2,136 | 507 |
| **Gross margin** | 48% | 44% | 39% | 27% | 29% |
| | | | | | |
| **Operating expenses** | | | | | |
| Fulfillment | 10,769 | 9,030 | 6,160 | 1,774 | 48 |
| Marketing | 15,280 | 13,411 | 21,613 | 18,077 | 795 |
| General and administrative | 14,598 | 15,423 | 11,741 | 5,832 | 1,231 |
| Total operating expenses | 40,647 | 37,864 | 39,514 | 25,683 | 2,074 |
| **Loss from operations** | (7,165) | (13,542) | (26,749) | (23,547) | (1,567) |
| **Operating margin** | −10% | −24% | −82% | −293% | −89% |
| | | | | | |
| Interest income | 160 | 459 | 1,424 | 510 | 0 |
| Interest expense | (706) | (1,036) | (1,124) | (201) | (1) |
| **Net income (loss)** | (7,711) | (14,109) | (26,449) | (23,238) | (1,568) |
| **Net margin** | −11.0% | −25.3% | −81.2% | −289.2% | −88.9% |

**Summary Balance Sheet Data**

(in thousands)

| At March 30 | 2003 | 2002 | 2001 | 2000 | 1999 |
|---|---|---|---|---|---|
| Cash and equivalents | 4,997 | 4,910 | 11,248 | 14,842 | 1,723 |
| Working capital | 7,179 | 483 | 19,087 | 14,982 | 1,155 |
| Total assets | 22,126 | 18,482 | 32,951 | 21,237 | 1,847 |
| Capital lease obligations | 1,775 | 477 | 661 | 776 | – |
| Total indebtedness | 1,123 | 6,000 | 6,797 | 6,614 | – |
| Stockholders' equity (deficit) | (71,451) | (64,191) | (51,439) | (25,513) | (1,997) |

*Source: RedEnvelope Form S-1, filed with the Securities and Exchange Commission on September 24, 2003.*

Like other successful e-commerce ventures, RedEnvelope has been able to achieve economies of scale and operations as revenues grew rapidly. Overall, in 2003, RedEnvelope achieved a –10% operating margin and a –11% net margin, vast improvements over earlier years such as 2000 when the net margin was –289%! These results are primarily due to the fact that RedEnvelope's marketing expenses and general and administrative expenses did not expand as rapidly as net revenues over the past few years. Looking forward, the history suggests that RedEnvelope will be profitable on an annual basis in the next year or two with positive net margins, assuming, of course, that it can maintain current revenue growth with only modest increases in marketing expense.

Looking at RedEnvelope's balance sheet, the company is relatively debt free. At March 30, 2003 it had $22 million in total assets and only $1.1 million in total indebtedness. RedEnvelope also had a strong working capital position of more than $7 million, which suggests that it is in a good position to cover current liabilities. These numbers do not reflect the impact of its recent initial public offering. RedEnvelope's IPO added to its capital assets by more than $35 million and as of the end of December 2003 it had total assets of $58 million. The company currently has a market capitalization of around $120 million and sells for about $15 a share, slightly above its offering price of $14. The company has a number of well-known Silicon Valley venture capital firms as investors, including W. R. Hambrecht and Sequoia Capital.

## STRATEGIC ANALYSIS: BUSINESS STRATEGY

The success of RedEnvelope will depend on management's ability to keep growing revenues, as well as its ability to successfully invest the $35 million in investor capital it has received from the recent IPO. Can a pure gift company on the Web continue to grow revenues at 25% forever? Or will RedEnvelope ultimately hit a growth ceiling and be forced to consider selling itself to a larger, more general-purpose online retailer that has more uniform year-round sales?

To keep growing at a rate roughly equal to the growth of all retail on the Internet (about 25% a year), RedEnvelope's management has adopted several strategies. First, it is seeking to strengthen its brand image through targeted promotions and advertisements, customizing promotions with strategic corporate partners, and continuing production of distinctive, high-quality, richly photographed catalogs. Second, the firm is seeking to expand its offering of unique products that cannot be found anywhere else (and that command much higher margins). Finally, the firm is attempting to achieve new operational efficiencies at its fulfillment center and to increase the efficiency of advertising. It remains to be seen if these efforts will result in 25% annual revenue growth over the next five years.

# STRATEGIC ANALYSIS: TECHNOLOGY

RedEnvelope uses third-party information technology systems for order fulfillment, merchandising, and financial reporting. The company developed its Web-store internally and integrated it with these other systems. The company continually makes improvements to the overall technology infrastructure to improve the shopping experience and order fulfillment capabilities. It currently uses Mail Order and Catalog System (MACS is widely used throughout the online retail industry) as its back-end order and fulfillment system. RedEnvelope's information technology systems are housed in a leased third-party facility in Santa Clara, California. Currently, RedEnvelope uses 28 servers to run its Web site. Data is stored in a database that runs on a redundant server and storage array. It also has standby servers that can provide additional capacity as necessary.

Like all pure online retailers, RedEnvelope is almost totally dependent on its Web site for efficient and uninterrupted operation of its business. The company's systems and operations—located in an active earthquake zone—are vulnerable to damage or interruption from power outages, computer and telecommunications failures, computer viruses, security breaches, and catastrophic events. The company's servers are located at the facilities of third-party service providers over which it has no direct control. In the event that the service provider experiences any interruption in its operations or ceases operations for any reason, or if the company is unable to agree on satisfactory terms for a continued hosting relationship, the company might experience a disruption in service or greatly increased costs of operation.

RedEnvelope—like many online retailers—is attempting to address the fact that more than 50% of online shoppers do not find what they want when visiting retail sites. One solution is complimentary personal shopping services that give site visitors an experience similar to that of real physical stores where sales people hold the hands of consumers and provide advice and personal attention. Lands' End, which introduced its personal shopper service in 2000, says that people who use the online personal shopper are 80% more likely to buy something compared to nonusers. On a RedEnvelope competitor site, FindGift.com, shoppers who use its "Advanced Gift Finder" service generate three times as much revenue as the average customer. RedEnvelope has two types of personalized shopping: live online chat or direct telephone support by a sales representative at the company's call center near Los Angeles. Both types of personal shopping support, executives believe, are far better than automated shopping bots based on visitors filling out forms (Schatz, 2003).

## STRATEGIC ANALYSIS: SOCIAL AND LEGAL CHALLENGES

The firm faces two legal challenges at this time. Since 2000, a UK company called Red Letter Days has disputed RedEnvelope's efforts to register its trademark in England and the European Community. Red Letter Days has refused offers of an amicable settlement. This does not mean that RedEnvelope cannot do business in Europe, but it does mean that RedEnvelope cannot register its trademarks there, and if it does do significant business in Europe, it would be open to legal challenges in the countries where Red Letter Days does business. If RedEnvelope were denied the opportunity to do business in Europe, this restriction could put a significant cap on the company's future growth potential.

In May 2003, RedEnvelope received notice from Activ8Now that RedEnvelope was violating two patents for online commerce held by Activ8Now. Like many online merchants facing such warnings, RedEnvelope is cautiously evaluating the claims, and it is unclear at this time how the company will respond. The company believes Activ8Now claims will not have a material negative impact on the company.

# FUTURE PROSPECTS

RedEnvelope has developed a strong brand name and an easy-to-use and pleasant Web site for gift hunting, and as a result, the company has emerged as one of the top online gift stores in 2004. The firm has several strong competitors such as 1StopGiftShop.com and FindGift.com, as well as general retailers who emphasize "gifting" opportunities, such as Amazon.com, Macy's and Bloomingdales online stores, Pottery Barn, Brookstone, Sharper Image, Tiffany, Harry & David, and 1-800-Flowers, to mention just a few. In this environment it would seem difficult for RedEnvelope to truly differentiate itself from direct competitors, forcing the company to rely increasingly on the brand awareness of its red gift boxes, truly unique products, and execution of customer orders. To continue rapid growth, RedEnvelope management will have to explore the opportunities for developing strategic alliances with online portals and well-established general merchandisers such as Amazon and eBay.

On December 28, 2003, RedEnvelope reported that it would likely have $35 million in revenue for the quarter rather than $40 million, nearly a 10% drop from expectations. Net income would be a paltry $1 million in the third quarter rather than the predicted $4.3 million. The problem was that management underestimated demand for its products, and was unable to fill orders because of lack of inventory. RedEnvelope's problems were made worse because it designs many of its products and personalizes others. Unlike most online vendors who sell commodity products, RedEnvelope has a very thin supply chain. The company cited the difficulty of obtaining enough inventory of its unique items and a slower than expected ability to create customized products with monograms and logos. Both developments resulted in larger than expected customer order cancelations. RedEnvelope's stock plunged to a post-IPO low of $9.71. Other specialty item stores such as Sharper Image did not report such difficulties.

These recent difficulties highlight the challenges management faces. RedEnvelope will have to develop more reliable supply chain relationships in order to guarantee that the unusual gifts shown in the catalog and online stores in fact can be obtained. One quality of truly unique products is that they are made by small firms in small lots. If a truly unique item becomes popular at

RedEnvelope, inventory is likely to be quickly depleted. The firm will also have to invest heavily in more sophisticated order fulfillment and personalization technology to avoid high levels of customer order cancellation.

## SOURCES

Barker, Robert. "A Peek Inside RedEnvelope's IPO." *BusinessWeek Online*, September 15, 2003.

Flynn, Laurie. "Red Envelope, a Web Retailer, Is Too Popular for Its Own Good." *New York Times*, January 19, 2004.

RedEnvelope Inc. Form S-1 filed with the Securities and Exchange Commission on September 24, 2003.

Schatz, Elizabeth. "Testing Online Personal Shoppers." *Wall Street Journal*, December 16, 2003.

Wilson, Gretchen. "RedEnvelope Slashes Outlook, Citing Distribution Problems." *Wall Street Journal*, January 9, 2004.

# InsWeb and the Online Insurance Market

InsWeb Corporation operates an online insurance marketplace that enables consumers to comparison shop online and obtain insurance company-sponsored quotes for a variety of insurance products, including automobile, term life, and homeowners insurance. Founded in 1995 in the early years of e-commerce, by 2003 InsWeb had revenues of $24 million, up from a mere $3 million in 1998.

The U.S. insurance market is about $430 billion in 2004, and online insurance accounts for about $3 billion. There is plenty of room for online insurance to grow, but growth has been slow, much slower than earlier visionaries for online insurance had hoped.

InsWeb operates as a Web intermediary between insurance companies and the consumer. For the consumer, InsWeb aggregates the insurance offerings of many insurance companies at a single site, permitting the consumer to comparison shop. For insurance carriers, InsWeb aggregates customers at a single site and provides the companies with valuable sales leads. InsWeb has combined extensive knowledge of the insurance industry, technological expertise, and close relationships with a significant number of large insurance companies to develop an integrated online marketplace.

InsWeb's online marketplace enables consumers to research insurance-related topics, search for, analyze, and compare insurance products, apply for and receive insurance company-sponsored quotes for actual coverage, and purchase automobile insurance coverage through InsWeb's insurance agency. About 3 million consumers sought auto insurance quotes at InsWeb's Web site in 2003.

## THE VISION

InsWeb was the brainchild of Hussan Enan, son of an Egyptian insurance entre-preneur and a lifelong insurance industry salesman and executive. Enan knew nothing of the Internet or the Web until in 1994 his son introduced him to a pre-Internet network called Prodigy. His son was purchasing CDs online and pre-ferred to do so rather than go to the mall. His son showed Enan how to search Prodigy for insurance products. He found only one insurance offering: camp-ing gear insurance offered by Continental. The idea for InsWeb was born. The first idea was to build software that insurance companies could sell to their customers to help them purchase insurance. This idea flopped. Enan's second idea was to build software that would allow consumers to fill out a single online form and then receive quotes from participating insurance companies. InsWeb would receive revenue from sending leads to insurance carriers. By 1999, InsWeb had over forty large insurance carriers signed up, including the top four: State Farm, Allstate, Farmers, and Nationwide.

However, by 1999, InsWeb also realized that this model was not producing profits. In addition to acting as an e-marketplace, a sort of online insurance mall where consumers could comparison shop, InsWeb began selling its own insurance policies directly to consumers. InsWeb's cyberagency would of course compete directly with the agents of the insurance carriers it represented. Most insurance in the United States is sold through over 70,000 insurance agents, working either as independents or as employees for the carriers. Upstart insur-ance carriers GEICO and Progressive, the two fastest-growing carriers in the last decade, eliminated independent agents and sell directly over the phone or Internet to consumers. By 2000, InsWeb had many online insurance competi-tors such as Quotesmith.com, eBix.com (a reverse auction site), and esurance.com, as well as competition from national carriers such as Progressive and GEICO (competing mostly in the online auto insurance business). In addi-tion, the repeal of the Glass-Steagall Act in 1999 permitted banks, online and offline, to sell insurance products.

In 2000, InsWeb lost one of its largest insurers, State Farm, in part because of the inherent conflict with InsWeb's new cyberagency capability. However the other carriers remained with InsWeb.

In general, growth in the online insurance market has been strong, moving from $1 million in revenues in 1998 to over $13 billion in 2004. Yet the growth has been far less rapid than experts hoped. Consumers have not flocked to any of the insurance sites, and with the exception of auto insurance, which is more standardized than other policy lines, for most lines of insurance consumers may do some online shopping but complete insurance transactions via telephone or in face-to-face interactions with sales people. The reason is the actual and perceived complexity of insurance policies, the great diversity of offerings among hundreds of carriers, and the absence of industry standards for expressing the terms of policies. Briefly, insurance policies are designed to be so difficult to sell that a human sales person is required.

Despite the modest growth in the online insurance industry, reflected in the revenue growth of InsWeb (described later), InsWeb has been able to raise significant capital from venture capital investors such as SoftBank ($65 million) and insurance carriers such as Nationwide and CAN, each of which own about 11% of InsWeb. InsWeb's IPO in 1999 raised additional capital.

# BUSINESS MODEL

There are many possible business models for insurance on the Web. Single insurance companies can sell a broad range of their products directly to consumers, reducing costs to consumers and increasing convenience. Web-based information delivery provided by third-parties and intermediaries can provide information to consumers about insurance costs, although they cannot arrange directly for an insurance quote or policy. Another possibility is for insurance agencies that traditionally sell policies from many different carriers to go online. Still another possibility with the repeal of the Glass-Steagel Act is for integrated financial service firms such as E*Trade or CitiBank to offer insurance online as a part of their financial services package.

InsWeb's model initially was unique because it was based on the consumer filling in a standard form with information, communicating the information to insurance carrier information systems, and returning within seconds a valid, firm quotation for a policy. But in 2002, InsWeb added to its initial business model by directly selling insurance in ten states as an insurance agent representing 12 insurance companies.

InsWeb generates revenue primarily from transaction fees it charges the more than 45 insurance carriers with whom it has "instant quoting carrier" relationships. The company also generates revenue from insurance commissions it charges when it sells directly to the consumer as an insurance agent through its subsidiary, InsWeb Insurance Service Inc. In addition, the company receives developer and maintenance fees from insurance carriers who pay InsWeb to develop the software interface between the carriers' mainframe customer systems and InsWeb's online systems.

## FINANCIAL ANALYSIS

A look at InsWeb's statement of operations takes us back to the "bad old" days of the Web and into the "good new" days of today's surviving e-commerce companies (Table 7-1). From 1998 to 1999, InsWeb's revenues exploded from $4.3 million to $21.8 million. The years 2000–2002 showed relatively flat to modest revenue growth, with about 7% annual growth. InsWeb experienced a slight decline in revenues in 2003, and is on track to generate approximately $25 to $26 million in total revenues in 2004, although recent forecasts suggest that this may not be quite attainable. InsWeb's stock price has tended to reflect the growing realization that online insurance is increasingly competitive and no longer a growth industry. In 1999, at the highpoint of e-commerce optimism, InsWeb's IPO shares opened at $16 and then sold as high as $44 a share. Since then the high price of shares has declined every year. The high share price was $26 in 2000, $12 in 2001, and $7 in 2002 and 2003. Currently InsWeb shares sell for $5 but have sold as low as $1.50 in the last 12 months.

A quick look at InsWeb's financials over the last five years shows that the company has steadily and dramatically improved its bottom line results, moving from a $50 million net loss in 2000, to a much smaller $4.5 million net loss in 2002, to a $1 million profit in 2003. The small 2002 loss would have been much larger were it not for a sale of $10 million in assets, and the $1 million

| Table 7-1 | InsWeb Consolidated Statements of Operations and Summary Balance Sheet Data, 1999–2003 |

| Consolidated Statements of Operations | | (in thousands) | | | |
|---|---|---|---|---|---|
| For the fiscal year ended December 31 | 2003 | 2002 | 2001 | 2000 | 1999 |
| **Revenues** | | | | | |
| Transaction fees | 23,192 | 24,107 | 22,976 | 19,561 | 19,147 |
| Development and maintenance fees | 939 | 1,448 | 1,880 | 3,649 | 1,159 |
| Total revenues | 24,131 | 25,555 | 24,856 | 23,210 | 21,841 |
| **Operating expenses** | | | | | |
| Technology | 9,014 | 10,322 | 14,041 | 22,890 | 17,778 |
| Sales and marketing | 16,225 | 18,329 | 28,821 | 34,020 | 30,413 |
| General and administrative | 5,883 | 6,850 | 7,345 | 11,207 | 7,631 |
| Amortization of intangible assets | – | – | – | 1,150 | 3,129 |
| Amortization of stock-based compensation | – | – | 256 | 912 | 1,272 |
| Impairment of long-lived assets | – | (1) | 3,707 | 18,519 | 4,418 |
| Restructuring charges | – | (2) | 1,800 | 1,843 | 2,167 |
| Total operating expenses | 31,122 | 41,008 | 70,825 | 76,764 | 60,223 |
| **Income/loss from operations** | **(6,991)** | **(15,453)** | **(45,969)** | **(53,554)** | **(38,382)** |
| **Operating margin** | **−29%** | **−60%** | **−185%** | **−231%** | **−176%** |
| Interest expense | (86) | (465) | (1,043) | (87) | (1,229) |
| Interest and other income | 8,123 | 729 | 2,086 | 4,429 | 3,410 |
| Income/loss before change in accounting | 1046 | (15,189) | (44,926) | (49,212) | (36,201) |
| Cumulative effect of change in accounting | – | – | – | – | (1,635) |
| Extraordinary gain | – | 10,611 | – | – | – |
| **Net income/loss** | **1,046** | **(4,578)** | **(44,926)** | **(50,847)** | **(36,201)** |
| **Net margin** | **4%** | **−18%** | **−181%** | **−219%** | **−166%** |
| **Summary Balance Sheet Data** | | | | | |
| | | (in thousands) | | | |
| At December 31 | 2003 | 2002 | 2001 | 2000 | 1999 |
| Cash and cash equivalents | 15,223 | 12,382 | 14,627 | 24,795 | 25,689 |
| Short-term investments | 10,868 | 16,541 | 20,936 | 26,331 | 64,063 |
| Total current assets | 27,882 | 32,391 | 39,404 | 57,913 | 96,993 |
| Total assets | 29,882 | 37,692 | 54,342 | 73,008 | 118,281 |
| Total current liabilities | 5,603 | 10,604 | 9,080 | 6,256 | 5,631 |
| Long-term liabilities, excluding current portion | – | – | 13,490 | 1,312 | 1,464 |
| Total stockholders' equity | 24,279 | 27,088 | 31,772 | 63,884 | 111,185 |

Sources: "InsWeb Reports Fourth Quarter and Year-End Financial Results," InsWeb Press Release, February 4, 2004; InsWeb Form 10-K for the fiscal year ended December 31, 2002, filed with the Securities and Exchange Commission on March 27, 2003.

profit in 2003 would have been a $7 million dollar loss if not for a gain of $6.8 million realized on the sale of its remaining investment in Finance All KK, a Japanese company. Still, the financial picture improved greatly in 2002–2003.

In the early years up through 2001, marketing costs actually exceeded total revenues! Finally, by 2002, the company reined in the marketing costs and reduced general and administrative expenses, leading to a total cut in operating expenses of nearly 50%. Total operating expenses went from $76 million in the salad days of 2000 down to a leaner and meaner $41 million in 2002, and were further reduced to $31 million in 2003. Net margins have improved from –219% in 2000 to a more hopeful –18% in 2002, and a positive 4% in 2003.

Looking at results for 2003 suggests that InsWeb's dietary regimen of reduced marketing expenditure and administrative leanness are continuing to grow revenue modestly, and have helped to reduce the overall operating loss to the $7 million range compared to $15 million in 2002.

InsWeb's balance sheet bears the marks of an early e-commerce darling. It had amassed $118 million in assets in 1999, but by 2003 the assets had dropped to $29 million. Still, the company has enough assets to last for another three years at current rates of loss and perhaps much longer if it can achieve consistent break-even operations.

# STRATEGIC ANALYSIS: BUSINESS STRATEGIES

Since InsWeb was founded in 1995, the world of e-commerce and financial services has changed greatly. In 1995, the stodgy traditional insurance companies were largely oblivious to the Internet and e-commerce, and banking and brokerage firms could not sell insurance. In this period, InsWeb—and other early pioneers—were truly innovative in creating an online comparative shopping site where consumers could actually arrange for a policy entirely online. However, as Enan, the founder himself, notes, only about a third of InsWeb site visitors actually attempt to obtain a policy online, and of those, about one-third quit when they are asked to supply personal information. The fear of Internet privacy invasion and lack of trust, as well as policy complexity, have slowed the growth of online insurance. In addition, the competitive environment has changed, permitting many financial services to sell insurance directly.

InsWeb has attempted to elaborate its business model and develop new sources of revenue. Currently 80% of its revenues come from auto insurance, and InsWeb is attempting to broaden the types of insurance that carriers offer online. Four carriers account for approximately 60% of its revenue, which makes the company very dependent on a few large carriers. There is little management can do about this situation. Perhaps the most important new strategy is to grow the insurance agency business and derive new revenues from insurance commissions, in the process becoming an online "superagency." Another strategy pursued earlier is to build alliances with other financial service Web sites as well as general portals and seek to become the sole provider of insurance quotes on those sites. Currently InsWeb has such relationships with Yahoo!, MSN, and AOL. Consumers click on an insurance quote button and are brought to the InsWeb site.

In January 2001, InsWeb acquired the online insurance shopping and purchasing service operated by Intuit Insurance Services, Inc. Intuit produces the tax preparation software Quicken and promotes its software and tax services through its Web site Quicken.com. With its purchase of insurance quote assets from Intuit, InsWeb became the exclusive distributor of insurance quotes at the Quicken Web site.

## STRATEGIC ANALYSIS: COMPETITION

InsWeb has many competitors, which range from small online start-up companies to huge insurance carriers. Online ventures such as Quotesmith.com (doing business online as Insure.com) offers insurance quotes from more than 200 carriers and has a business model virtually identical to InsWeb. Quotesmith is about one-half the size of InsWeb. Another online start-up competitor is eBix.com. eBix.com advertises itself as "the only e-commerce portal for insurance on the Internet. It is designed for both consumers and insurance professionals offering a one-stop site for all kinds of insurance content." (www.ebix.com, 2004) In fact, eBix is a software company that creates agency management software and also software that connects online customers to back-office systems of major insurance carriers. In other words, eBix—like InsWeb—enables insurance carriers to sell on the Web without having to build their own proprietary systems. Both eBix and Quotesmith reported slow growth in 2003.

## STRATEGIC ANALYSIS: TECHNOLOGY

InsWeb faces a number of technological risks. Since launching its online marketplace, InsWeb has experienced occasional minor system failures or outages that have resulted in the online marketplace being out of service for a period ranging from several minutes to three hours. The performance, reliability, and availability of its Web site, quote-generating systems, and network infrastructure are critical to the company's reputation and its ability to attract a high volume of traffic and to attract and retain participating insurance companies.

The company's computer hardware operations are located in leased facilities in Gold River, California. A third-party service provider maintains a full backup system. If both locations experienced a system failure, the performance of the company's Web site would be harmed.

Several participating insurance companies have chosen a technical solution that requires that the company's Web-site servers communicate with the insurance companies' computer systems in order to perform the underwriting, risk analysis, and rating functions required to generate quotes. Thus, the availability of quotes from a given insurance company may depend in large part on the reliability of the insurance company's computer systems, over which InsWeb has no control. A malfunction in an insurance company's computer system or in the Internet connection between InsWeb's Web-site servers and the insurance company's system, or an excess of data traffic on the insurance company's system, could result in a delay in the delivery of e-mail quotes or could cause an insurance company that provides instant quotes to go offline until the problem was remedied. Any technological problems with or interruption of communications with an insurance company's computer systems could materially reduce the number of competing insurance companies available to provide quotes and therefore the level of service perceived by consumers on the online marketplace.

---

## STRATEGIC ANALYSIS: SOCIAL AND LEGAL CHALLENGES

In February 2001, InsWeb temporarily suspended its online health insurance quoting services due to the decision by eHealthInsurance, Inc., formerly InsWeb's exclusive provider of online health insurance quotes, to unilaterally terminate their marketing agreement. In February 2001, eHealthInsurance filed suit in the U.S. District Court for the Northern District of California, alleging InsWeb's failure to perform its obligations under the agreement. In March 2001, InsWeb filed a counterclaim alleging that eHealthInsurance wrongfully terminated the agreement and pursued a course of conduct aimed at damaging InsWeb's business. On March 24, 2003, the parties agreed to settle the lawsuit and dismiss all claims asserted against each other. In addition, eHealthInsurance agreed to pay InsWeb $800,000 for the services performed by InsWeb prior to the termination of the agreement.

Like many other firms that had IPOs in the late 1990s, InsWeb is the defendant in a class action securities lawsuit brought on behalf of all persons who purchased InsWeb shares from 1999 to 2000. The suit alleges that InsWeb and its underwriters violated the Securities Act of 1933 and the Securities Exchange Act of 1934, on the grounds that its prospectus failed to disclose, among other things, that (1) the underwriters had solicited and received excessive and undisclosed commissions from certain investors in exchange for which the underwriters allocated to those investors substantial blocks of the stock sold in the initial public offering and (2) the underwriters had entered into agreements with customers whereby the underwriters agreed to allocate shares of the stock sold in the initial public offering to those customers in exchange for which the customers agreed to purchase additional shares of InsWeb stock in the after-market at predetermined prices that were above the initial public offering price. No specific damages were claimed. In February 2003, the court dismissed the claims alleging violations of the Securities Exchange Act of 1934 but allowed the plaintiffs to proceed with the remaining claims. InsWeb believes that the remaining allegations against InsWeb and its current and former officers and directors are without merit, and the company intends to contest the claims vigorously. The litigation is in the preliminary stage, and at this time, InsWeb cannot predict its outcome. An unfavorable outcome could have a material adverse effect on InsWeb's financial condition, results of operations, and cash flows.

# FUTURE PROSPECTS

The days of a stand-alone pure online insurance quotation site may be over. While the online insurance market is still growing at double-digit rates, 90% of this growth is in auto insurance. None of the pure online insurance sites are showing double-digit growth. Indeed, most are showing flat revenue growth during 2002–2003, as has InsWeb. Where has the online insurance growth occurred? Banks and brokerage firms, now entering the insurance carrier business, are offering insurance online at their own sites in direct competition with InsWeb, Insure.com, and eBix. In addition, the major carriers along with low-cost carriers such as GEICO and Progressive, both with a long history of selling direct to consumers without agents, are also showing strong online sales growth.

Clearly InsWeb needs a new business model selling a more diverse range of insurance products and a more diverse range of financial products. The challenge facing management is how to grow revenues in the traditional insurance business while at the same time reaching out to new sources of revenue. Becoming an online superagency generating commission revenues is one path to growth. Beyond that, InsWeb management will have to consider adding other financial services such as retirement planning, college financial planning, or other savings programs in order to attract a much larger Web audience and resume double-digit growth.

## SOURCES

Hoovers's Online. "InsWeb Corporation Fact Sheet." March 18, 2004.

"InsWeb Reports Fourth Quarter and Year-End Financial Results," InsWeb Press Release, February 4, 2004.

InsWeb Form 10-K for the fiscal year ended December 31, 2002, filed with the Securities and Exchange Commission on March 27, 2003.

"Quotesmith.com Revises 2003 Fincl Guidance, Issues Guidance for 2004." WSJ.com, December 12, 2003.

www.eBix.com, "About ebix." March 18, 2004.

# WebMD:

## Rx for the Nation's Medical Ills?

No other site on the Web equals WebMD as a popular brand-name destination for health and health care information, both for general health consumers and for practicing doctors. WebMD is one of the most successful B2C content providers on the Web, dispensing health information to millions of doctors and health-conscious consumers. But the public Web presence of WebMD (www.webmd.com) is a small part of a much larger B2B business that connects health care providers (doctors, dentists, clinics, and hospitals) with health care payers (insurance companies, HMOs, health care plans, and employers). In 2003, WebMD had nearly $1 billion in revenues, 5,600 employees, and a market capitalization of nearly $3 billion. However, since beginning operations in 1996, the company has lost money every year and has a cumulative deficit of $10.2 billion.

WebMD (formerly Healtheon/WebMD) offers a number of services to electronically connect physicians, hospitals, pharmacies, insurance providers, and consumers in a transaction-based environment. Its transaction services encompass such tasks as HMO enrollment, referrals, data retrieval, and claims processing. WebMD's Medical Manager software helps physicians, dentists, and other health care professionals to run their practices. In addition, WebMD maintains a Web site offering both consumers and physicians a variety of health-related information services including access to medical literature, news, and features, as well as message boards, newsletters, online shopping, and other typical Web portal features.

Wall Street analysts estimate the total annual market for WebMD services at around $175 billion, and that WebMD has to date garnered only 1% of that market, suggesting a very large upside opportunity for future growth. In the United States in 2004, the health care industries account for $1.6 trillion in GDP, making it one of the largest single industries in the country. Health care is also one of the fastest-growing industries as the population ages, expensive new drugs come to market, and demand for health care explodes. Analysts believe health care is one of the worst-managed sectors in the United States, a sector where more than one-third of the annual expenditure (about $500 billion) goes to the administration of a Byzantine bureaucracy that relies almost entirely on paper-based forms, fax machines, and redundant data collection.

## THE VISION

WebMD started life in 1996 as Healtheon Corporation. Healtheon was the third billion-dollar (market capitalization) Internet company created by Web innovator Jim Clark. The first $2 billion companies were Silicon Graphics (an early leading animation company that produced the computers used to create the special effects for films such as the *Star Wars* films) and Netscape (the first commercially successful Web browser). While Silicon Graphics and Netscape were both unable to maintain their market leadership, WebMD has retained its leadership position in health care information services.

The original idea behind Healtheon was to cut out the bureaucracy and expense of America's health care system by creating a Web site where health care providers (doctors, dentists, clinics, hospitals, and others) could meet the health care payers (insurance companies, government agencies, and employers). The idea was to leverage the capabilities of the Web to streamline administrative and clinical processes, promote efficiency, and reduce costs by facilitating information exchange, communication, and electronic transactions between health care participants. To a large extent, the company has succeeded in this mission even as it has had a difficult time showing a profit.

Healtheon grew from an idea to a billion-dollar company through seven key acquisitions, beginning in 1999 with the acquisition of WebMD for $3.6 billion. Perhaps its most important acquisition, however, has been the purchase of

Envoy for $2.4 billion in January 2000. Envoy was a pioneer in the development of EDI (electronic data interchange) in the health care industry. Other acquisitions that strengthened Healtheon's position as a leading medical transaction processing service included MedE America (1999), Medcast (1999), Kinetra (2000), OnHealth (2000), and MedicalManager (2000). The acquisition spree ended with the decline of the stock market in spring 2000, although the company continued to make many smaller acquisitions in 2003 as its share price rose to $10.

The underlying economics supporting the transition to standard electronic medical transaction payments in the United States is compelling. A typical paper-based medical transaction (such as a patient visiting a doctor's office or being admitted to a hospital) costs $5 to $6, but the cost of the same transaction on an electronic platform is less than $1. At WebMD, the average cost of a transaction is just 21 cents. If the entire United States medical system converted to electronic transaction platforms, the total savings are estimated to exceed $73 billion, according to the Medical Group Management Association.

## BUSINESS MODEL

WebMD has four business segments: transaction services (WebMD Envoy) ($506 million in 2003), physician services (WebMD Practice Services) ($303 million), portal services (WebMD Health) ($111 million), and plastic technologies (Porex)($72 million). Each segment has a different business model. The largest segment, transaction services, provides electronic transactions between health care payers and physicians, pharmacies, dentists, hospitals, laboratory companies, and other health care providers. The company generates revenue in this segment by selling transaction services to health-care payers and providers, generally on either a per transaction basis or, in the case of some providers, on a monthly fixed fee basis. The company also generates revenue by selling patient statement services, typically on a per statement basis. A significant portion of WebMD Envoy revenues come from the country's leading national and regional health-care payers.

The value proposition to its medical industry companies is that WebMD Envoy can provide transaction services and management at a far lower cost than can individual firms as a result of scale economies of its software and hardware base. WebMD electronic transactions significantly reduce processing time and costs, compared to mail, fax, or telephone, and increase productivity for both payers and providers. The transactions facilitated by WebMD include administrative transactions (such as claims submission and status inquiry, eligibility and patient coverage verification, referrals and authorizations, and electronic remittance advice, and clinical transactions, such as lab test ordering and reporting of results) and automated patient billing services to providers (including statement printing and mailing). The company is attempting to increase the percentage of health care transactions that are handled electronically and to sell new value-added services to providers and payers.

In its physician services (WebMD Practices Services) segment, the company's leading product brands are WebMD Medical Manager, Intergy, ULTIA, and Medical Manager Network Services. These systems provide administrative and financial applications that enable health care providers and their administrative personnel to manage their practices more efficiently, and electronic medical record and other clinical applications that assist them in delivering patient care. These provider systems are linked to WebMD's Envoy transaction services.

Customers can purchase a base system and then add additional modules and services over time to expand their use of state-of-the-art technology as needed. Alternatively, small practices can purchase services hosted by WebMD and avoid the costs of local computer servers entirely. The company generates revenue in this segment from one-time fees for licenses to their software modules and system hardware and from recurring fees for the maintenance and support of software and system hardware. Pricing depends on the number and type of software modules to be licensed, the number of users, the complexity of the installation, and other factors. The products and services are priced on a monthly fee per user basis or a per transaction basis.

In its portal services (WebMD Health) segment, the company's WebMD Health portal (webmd.com) offers a variety of online resources and services for consumers and health care professionals. For consumers, the WebMD site provides information about wellness, diseases, and treatments. The company's Medscape portal service is aimed at physicians and provides medical news, chat groups, conference summaries, and medical education. The company generates revenue in this segment by selling advertising, selling sponsorships of specific pages, sections, or events, and licensing content, as well as related software and services. Most of the revenue from this segment comes from a small number of very large medical and pharmaceutical companies, medical device companies, employers and health plans, and media distribution companies.

In its plastics technology (Porex) segment (WebMD's smallest's segment), the company develops, manufactures, and distributes proprietary porous and solid plastic products and components used in health care, industrial, and consumer applications. Porex manufactures porous and solid plastic products used in a diverse set of industries from plastic pens (porous pen tips) to medical membranes. Porex customers include both users of finished products and manufacturers, who include Porex components in products for the medical device, life science, research and clinical laboratory, surgical, and other markets. Porex is an international business with manufacturing operations in North America, Europe, and Asia and customers in more than 65 countries. WebMD attempted to sell off Porox for several years but abandoned those efforts in 2003.

## FINANCIAL ANALYSIS

When examining WebMD's financial performance, it is important to consider two periods: pre-2002 and post-2002. As seen in Table 8-1, the company's revenues grew explosively in the period 1998–2001 as the company acquired other companies.

Revenue moved from $102 million in 1999 to $842 million in 2001, an 825% increase. An analysis of segment growth patterns provides some insight into the company's future revenue growth prospects and suggests some future strategies for growth (Table 8-2).

Portal services, shows the strongest growth in 2003 (31.1%), while the largest segment, transaction services, shows much slower growth (8.3%).

An examination of WebMD's balance sheet reveals that it has weakened over the past few years as a result of significant losses from acquisitions and operations. Cash and cash equivalents fell from a high of over $500 million in

2000 to $190 million in 2002, with a slight rebound to $270 million in 2003. The company could continue to experience overall net losses in the $50 million range for about four years. It also maintains a comfortable cushion of around $200 million in working capital (the difference between total current

| Table 8-1 | WebMD Consolidated Statements of Operations and Summary Balance Sheet Data, 1999–2003 | | | | |
|---|---|---|---|---|---|
| **Consolidated Statements of Operations** | | | **(in thousands)** | | |
| For the fiscal year ended December 31 | 2003 | 2002 | 2001 | 2000 | 1999 |
| Revenue | 963,980 | 871,696 | 842,020 | 574,524 | 102,149 |
| **Costs and expenses** | | | | | |
| Cost of operations | 564,939 | 509,744 | 568,321 | 430,296 | 88,576 |
| Development and engineering | 42,985 | 43,467 | 43,572 | 59,957 | 29,669 |
| Sales, marketing, general and administrative | 282,482 | 283,424 | 448,082 | 535,462 | 82,315 |
| Depreciation, amortization and other | 62,434 | 125,593 | 2,394,857 | 2,188,461 | 193,067 |
| Legal expense | 3,959 | – | – | – | – |
| Impairment of long-lived and other assets | – | – | 3,816,115 | – | – |
| Total operating expenses | 956,799 | 1,011,384 | 7,333,277 | 3,229,735 | 393,627 |
| **Income/Loss from operations** | 7,181 | (85,507) | (6,432,249) | (2,638,133) | (291,478) |
| **Operating margin** | .7% | –9% | –714% | –446% | –285% |
| **Other Income (loss)** | | | | | |
| Restructuring and integration (benefit) charge | – | (5,850) | 266,755 | 452,919 | – |
| (Gain) loss on investments | (1,659) | (6,547) | – | 40,365 | – |
| Interest income | 22,901 | 19,590 | 30,409 | 51,467 | 4,013 |
| Interest expense | 15,214 | 8,491 | 507 | 735 | 527 |
| Other income, net | 4,218 | 3,844 | – | – | – |
| Income (loss) from continuing operations before income taxes | 20,745 | (63,192) | (6,665,780) | (3,082,114) | (287,992) |
| Income tax (benefit) provision | 4140 | (10,079) | 2,588 | 790 | – |
| Income (loss) from continuing operations | 16,605 | (53,113) | (6,668,368) | (3,082,114) | (287,992) |
| Incomes (loss) from discontinued operations | (33,611) | 3,411 | (3,950) | 1,296 | – |
| **Net Income/loss** | (17,006) | (49,702) | (6,672,318) | (3,081,608) | (287,992) |
| **Net margin** | –1.7% | –5% | –741% | –521% | –282% |

(continued)

| Table 8-1 | WebMD Consolidated Statements of Operations and Summary Balance Sheet Data, 1999–2003 (continued) |
|---|---|

**Summary Balance Sheet Data** (in thousands)

| At December 31: | 2003 | 2002 | 2001 | 2000 | 1999 |
|---|---|---|---|---|---|
| Current Assets | | | | | |
| Cash, cash equivalents, and short-term investments | 270,681 | 186,484 | 378,762 | 505,793 | 291,286 |
| Long-term marketable securities | 456,034 | 456,716 | 18,769 | 222,774 | – |
| Total current assets | 508,101 | 504,980 | 617,959 | 944,633 | 363,605 |
| Total assets | 2,135,306 | 1,766,248 | 1,601,454 | 8,487,108 | 4,123,668 |
| Total current liabilities | 305,528 | 311,949 | 327,091 | 338,386 | 147,301 |
| Convertible subordinated notes | 649,999 | 300,000 | – | – | – |
| Other long-term liabilities | 1,182 | 498 | 1,226 | 15,279 | 2,695 |
| Stockholders' equity | 1,178,597 | 1,153,801 | 1,255,512 | 8,097,435 | 3,973,672 |

*Sources: WebMD Corporation Form 10-K for the fiscal year ended December 31, 2003, filed with the Securities and Exchange Commission on March 15, 2004; WebMD Corporation Form 10-K for the fiscal year ended December 31, 2002, filed with the Securities and Exchange Commission on March 27, 2003.*

liabilities and total current assets). Total assets have been buoyed by a rising stock market. Its portfolio of stocks held in other companies has expanded greatly to over $450 million, and total assets have increased to $2.1 billion.

| Table 8-2 | WebMD Segment Revenues and Growth 2000–2002 |
|---|---|

| | % of Overall Revenue | | Total Revenue (in thousands) | | |
| Revenues | 2003* | % Growth/Decline 2003 vs. 2002 | 2003 | 2002 | 2001 |
|---|---|---|---|---|---|
| Transaction Services | 52.4% | 8.3% | 505.7 | 466.8 | 457.5 |
| Physician Services | 31.3% | 9.9% | 302.6 | 275.3 | 260.2 |
| Portal Services | 11.4% | 31.1% | 110.6 | 84.3 | 74.6 |
| Plastic technologies | 7.4% | –40% | 71.9 | 120 | 121 |
| Eliminations (net) | | | (26.9) | (20.5) | (12.2) |
| Net Revenue | | | 963.9 | 871.6 | 842 |

*\* The sum of these percentages exceeds 100% because certain of the revenue is from inter-segment transactions and is eliminated when WebMD consolidates its results.*

*Sources: WebMD Corporation Form 10-K for the fiscal year ended December 31, 2003, filed with the Securities and Exchange Commission on March 15, 2004.*

However its long-term obligations (convertible subordinated notes, issued mostly as bank debt and other long-term bond debt) have increased considerably in the last two years, to over $650 million. The balance sheet therefore has elements of long-term strength even though a significant part of this strength is the value of securities in its portfolio, which can change drastically in a very short time.

## STRATEGIC ANALYSIS: BUSINESS STRATEGY

WebMD's primary strategy is to grow the largest segment of its business-transaction services. WebMD acts as an independent medical information clearinghouse for payers and providers. The company is counting on significant future growth in this area largely because of the Healthcare Insurance Portability and Accountability Act of 1996 (HIPAA), which requires medical payers and providers to adopt common format and data standards for eight of the most common health care transactions (the so-called "transactions rule"). The transaction standards are to be developed by recognized standards publishing organizations. In addition, HIPAA requires that all electronic medical claims be handled in accordance with HIPAA privacy standards and HIPAA security standards. The rules for implementing the law were adopted in 2000, and larger providers and payers were required to implement the rules by October 2003.

To pursue the opportunities provided by HIPAA, WebMD acquired Medifax-EDI, a Nashville-based claims clearinghouse specializing in performing real-time eligibility checks on patients' medical coverage. Medifax-EDI has been growing at 25% annually for several years by helping doctors and hospitals identify a patient's insurance carrier at the moment of delivery of health services. The purchase price of $280 million was considered exceptionally high by many analysts, but management hopes to integrate Medifax-EDI into its Envoy EDI system to round out the portfolio of transaction services that WebMD and Envoy provide to doctors and hospitals.

In addition to HIPAA, WebMD is also counting heavily on the transition of the nation's health care providers (doctors and hospitals) to "electronic medical records" (EMR). Currently most providers rely on paper-based charts and written records, a costly alternative to electronic records. The physicians' services segment of WebMD has developed a suite of electronic medical record, document management, and portable hand-held computing solutions that make it possible for doctors and nurses to gain access to a patient's complete medical information anywhere in the hospital or clinic via wireless networks.

## STRATEGIC ANALYSIS: COMPETITION

In each of its segments, WebMD faces significant competitors. In transaction and clearinghouse services, its main direct competitors are NDCHealth Corporation, an Atlanta-based health-care information company that processes pharmacy claims; ProxyMed Inc., a firm that processes medical claims; and Quovadx Inc., a technology firm that produces software for providers to connect their own network to insurance payer systems.

Perhaps the most significant competitors to WebMD clearinghouse services are its own larger customers. Currently, WebMD is counting on the large and most profitable players with millions of transactions to pay WebMD a transaction service fee for providing the service. However, these large provider and payer institutions can also create their own networks to one another and eliminate the WebMD clearinghouse. That would leave WebMD with the smaller customers, which are the least profitable.

## STRATEGIC ANALYSIS: TECHNOLOGY

WebMD relies in its largest segment transaction services on an EDI (electronic data interchange) technology platform to connect providers to payers. The Envoy platform is a proprietary platform built prior to the development of government-accepted standards for electronic documents in the medical arena required by HIPAA. As these new standards are adopted, WebMD will have to change its own EDI system to conform, and it will incur considerable expense. In addition, software firms such as Quovadx, Inc. are making it easier for large payers to develop direct links with providers. In both these areas, WebMDs technological leadership in providing a universal platform for the exchange of medical information is severely challenged. On the other hand, WebMD has the opportunity to develop a standards-based universal platform for medical information of greater scale and potential efficiency than most of its direct competitors.

## STRATEGIC ANALYSIS: SOCIAL AND LEGAL CHALLENGES

WebMD is involved in several shareholder lawsuits. In the first, shareholders argue that WebMD overpaid for Envoy in its 2000 acquisition due to inflated accounting statements by Envoy prior to its acquisition. The company has insurance that will pay for any losses in this litigation. Following WebMD's IPO (initial public offering), three shareholder suits have named WebMD as a defendant, although these suits are mostly directed at the underwriters Morgan Stanley and Company Incorporated and Goldman Sachs & Company. In these lawsuits, plaintiffs allege that IPO shares were allocated unfairly and in violation of the Securities and Exchange Act of 1934. In these cases the firm expects to be indemnified by the underwriters should it lose the judgment.

In September 2003, agents from the FBI and the Internal Revenue Service raided offices of WebMD in New Jersey and Florida as part of an inquiry into the company's software business and $5.5 million restatement of its 1999 revenues. The company's executives believe the raid and its results will not produce evidence of faulty or illegal accounting and will not affect revenue statements of subsequent years. However, they expect to incur potentially significant legal expenses in connection with the investigation, and in 2003, WebMD recorded a $4 million expense for legal fees.

## FUTURE PROSPECTS

WebMD management is under significant pressure to show growth in a new way in addition to buying the earnings of acquired companies. For the foreseeable future, WebMD is focused on primarily growing through internal improvements in revenues and reduced costs of existing businesses. Its fastest-growing segment, portal services, based on its popular portal sites for consumers and physicians, unfortunately is too small a part of the firm's overall revenue picture to make a significant impact. Moreover, this segment depends on a small number of very large providers and payers for advertising revenues. Although there is every reason to believe these advertisers will continue to pay advertising fees to gain access to WebMD's large, upscale, health-oriented audience, it is unlikely to be sufficient to aggressively grow the larger company.

In transaction services, managers are keenly aware that their growth strategy depends on two factors: (1) the rate at which medical payers and providers adopt HIPAA transaction standards and (2) the ability and willingness of large institutions to develop direct contacts with one another to share medical transaction data. Unfortunately, in the short term, medical institutions have been slow to adopt HIPAA standards even though they are required to do so by HIPAA. This go-slow attitude hurt revenues somewhat in 2003, but most analysts believe medical institutions will eventually comply with the law. Some Wall Street investors expect WebMD to build on its 10% revenue growth rate in 2003 and reach a more robust 20% rate in 2004. More worrisome for WebMD is the possibility that the standards' sword cuts two ways. The possibility exists that WebMD will lose its main competitive weapon—a proprietary EDI-based transaction clearing platform—as large medical providers and payers (assisted by the new industrywide standards) develop direct links with one another, cutting out the middleman—WebMD. Direct-exchange software platforms will increasingly be offered by software companies eager to enter the market once industry standards are widely adopted. In either event, the resulting competition will tend to drive transaction fees toward a very small number, and medical transaction processing could become a commodity business based on price alone. To avoid this outcome, WebMD will have to develop a broad range of electronic services for its large customers that go far beyond mere transaction processing. With its portal and physician services products, WebMD is well endowed to exceed in this larger marketplace.

## SOURCES

Bloomberg News. "WebMD Says Profit Will Be Below Forecast." October 14, 2003.

Freeman, Adam. "WebMD Seeks to Expand Into Claims Processing." *Wall Street Journal*, November 19, 2003.

Vendetti, Anthony. "Is WebMD the Rx for Your Portfolio?" *Barron's Online*, November 12, 2003.

WebMD Corporation Form 10-K for the fiscal year ended December 31, 2003, filed with the Securities and Exchange Commission on March 15, 2004.

WebMD Corporation Form 10-K for the fiscal year ended December 31, 2002, filed with the Securities and Exchange Commission on March 27, 2002.

# Ask Jeeves:

## The Butler Knows

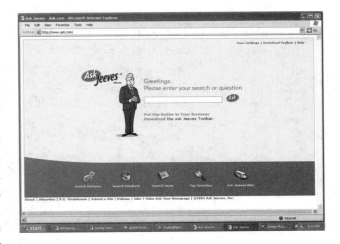

Ask Jeeves Inc., is a provider of Web-based search and self-service technologies aimed at creating a unique user experience that emphasizes ease of use, relevance, precision, and the opportunity for the user to learn. Ask Jeeves is the fifth largest search company behind Yahoo!, Google, Microsoft's MSN, and America Online (AOL). Each year about 13 million people visit Ask Jeeves' Web site, Ask.com, to ask "the Butler" (the Ask Jeeves search engine's mascot) to search the Web for a topic, product, person, or service. P. G. Wodehouse (1881–1975) was the creator of, among other characters, the original and immortal Jeeves (the archetypal "gentleman's gentleman") and his master Bertie Wooster. Wodehouse is widely regarded as one of the greatest humorists of the twentieth century and his work is read and loved by fans worldwide. Ask Jeeves licenses the Butler graphic from the P. G. Wodehouse Trust.

The search industry is currently going through a very rapid expansion driven by the fact that 80% of the Web's users navigate the Web through a search engine and that over 35% of all product searches on the Web begin with a search engine. The search industry discovered a few years ago that an ideal time to advertise to people is when they are looking for something. Thus was born the paid inclusion and "search engine marketing" business. Overture was the first search engine to charge advertisers to be listed in search results in 1998. By 2003 the market had taken off, growing 40% in 2003, and it now constitutes 23% of the $6 billion spent on Internet advertising. Because of the strength of the search engine advertising market, the fifth place Ask Jeeves stock advanced over 800% in 2003 from a low of $3 to a current level in the $20–$25 range.

## THE VISION

Ask Jeeves was founded in Berkeley, California, in late 1995, by Garrett Gruener and David Warthen. Gruener and Warthen envisioned a more humanized way to search the Web. The original vision of Ask Jeeves' founders was to create a search engine for ordinary people and even children that did not require the use of Boolean search arguments, odd characters, or other special language. Instead, Ask Jeeves based its search on parsing natural language questions from users, such as "What should I get my mother for Mother's Day?" Ask Jeeves' original technology parses users' questions or keywords to determine their likely topics of interest, and it analyzes relationships among Web sites devoted to those topics to determine which sites are likely to be the most authoritative. The original Ask Jeeves search algorithm therefore closely developed along with Google to focus on the popularity of a Web site to determine its relevance, as well as the so-called "natural language" interface. In response to a user's questions, Ask.com then delivers the following types of responses:

- Sponsored Web results (paid placement listings from advertisers)
- Related searches (a list of automatically generated hyperlinks to third-party Web sites, with the most relevant and authoritative Web sites listed first)
- Web results (listings generated by Ask Jeeves search engine based on relevance)
- A choice of Web product, picture, and news searches

When the user clicks on products, relevant products provided by PriceGrabber.com are listed. Ask Jeeves also has a syndicated relationship with Google in which user product searches are provided by Google and the fees from click-throughs are split with Google.

In late 2001, Ask Jeeves purchased Teoma.com, a Web search engine that uses an algorithm to rank the relevance of Web sites to a particular query on the basis of "Subject-Specific Popularity." Instead of focusing on the total number of links from any and all Web sites leading to a particular Web site as does Google and other search engines, Teoma analyzes the Web in terms of communities of similar subject-matter Web sites. For instance, it ranks a soccer Web site based on the number of links to it from other soccer Web sites, and places less emphasis on the number of links from general sports or other types of Web sites. Although it is difficult to say that the Teoma technique produces results superior to Google's, Teoma and Google were both given an A ranking in a recent test performed by *Search Engine Watch*.

## BUSINESS MODEL

Ask.com is the flagship Web property of the Ask Jeeves search network. Well known for its butler, Jeeves, this Web site provides a guided experience that helps users find the best answers to their questions on the Web. In addition to Ask.com, Ask Jeeves also operates three other Web sites: Ask.co.uk, a British counterpart to Ask.com, Ajkids.com, a child-friendly version of Ask.com, and Teoma.com, the home of the Teoma search technology used by all Ask Jeeves' Web sites. Together, these four sites attracted an audience of 29.9 million users who queried an estimated aggregate 7.5 million Web pages a day during the fourth quarter of 2003.

Prior to July 2003, the company did business through two divisions: the Web Properties division and the Jeeves Solutions division. The Web Properties division combines automated natural language-parsing software, topic-specific Web content analysis tools, and popularity-based search technology with advanced search algorithms to give Web users easy access to the information they seek. The Web Properties division delivers Web search results at Ask.com, Ask.co.uk, Teoma.com, and AJKids.com. It generates revenue in two ways. First, it syndicates search results and ad products to approximately 41 third-party Web sites, as of December 31, 2003, including portals, infomediaries, and content and destination Web sites. On these sites, Ask Jeeves provides its search engine technology and search results for a fee. The second source of Web Properties revenue derives from offering advertisers a variety of targeted tools for promoting their products to the Ask Jeeves user base. Types of advertising range from ubiquitous banner ads placed by its partner, DoubleClick, in response to user-initiated searches to more advanced pay-for-placement and keyword products, in which the company displays "Sponsored Web Results" composed of links paid for by advertisers. Ask Jeeves receives a fee for each user click-through.

In early 2003, Ask Jeeves decided to focus its business on the Web Properties division, and decided to sell its Jeeves Solutions division, which licensed the company's search engine technology to other companies for call center and customer management services. On July 1, 2003, it sold various assets of the Jeeves Solution division to Kanisa, Inc. for $3.4 million in cash, and a $750,000 promissory note.

In July 2002, the company entered into an agreement with Google, Inc., to participate in its sponsored links program. Under this agreement, Google sells paid placements to tens of thousands of advertisers, and Ask Jeeves displays Google's paid placements on Ask Jeeves U.S. Web sites. The company also syndicates Google's paid placements, together with search results, to third-party Web sites in the Ask Jeeves syndication network of portals and corporations. In exchange for making its Web traffic available to Google's advertisers, Ask Jeeves shares in the revenue generated from those advertisers.

In the year ended December 31, 2003, combined paid placement revenues from Google made up 55% of the company's revenues! The U.S. agreement with Google is scheduled to terminate in September 2005. Ask Jeeves also relies on third-party advertising services, provided by DoubleClick, Inc., to deliver advertisements to its users. The U.S. DoubleClick, Inc., agreement will expire on February 27, 2007.

Although Ask Jeeves is highly dependent on Google and DoubleClick for advertising revenue, at the same time Google and DoubleClick are eager to gain access to Ask Jeeves' 30 million online users. This was particularly true during the advertising downdraft of 2001–2002 and even more so now that Yahoo! (the Web's leading portal) has replaced Google as its search engine results provider now that Yahoo! has purchased Overture—the Web's largest paid placement search engine.

| Table 9-1 | Ask Jeeves Consolidated Statement of Operations and Summary Balance Sheet Data, 1999–2003 |

| Consolidated Statements of Operations | (in thousands) | | | | |
|---|---|---|---|---|---|
| For the fiscal year ending December 31 | 2003 | 2002 | 2001 | 2000 | 1999 |
| Revenues | 107,292 | 65,048 | 51,569 | 95,700 | 22,027 |
| Cost of revenues | 21,917 | 19,302 | 20,546 | 39,269 | 14,084 |
| Gross profit (loss) | 85,375 | 45,746 | 31,023 | 56,431 | 7,943 |
| Gross margin | 79.5% | 70.3% | 60% | 59% | 36% |
| | | | | | |
| Operating expenses | | | | | |
| Product development | 14,768 | 13,301 | 14,655 | 24,502 | 8,610 |
| Sales and marketing | 31,902 | 25,973 | 29,812 | 81,641 | 35,304 |
| General and administrative | 19,025 | 15,163 | 17,554 | 29,598 | 8,411 |
| Stock-based compensation | – | – | – | 2,996 | 3,936 |
| Amortization of goodwill | – | – | 22,823 | 82,624 | |
| Write-off of in-process technology | – | – | – | 11,652 | 544 |
| Acquisition costs | – | – | – | – | 6,045 |
| Impairment of long-lived assets | 702 | 2,592 | 355,183 | – | – |
| Restructuring costs | – | 1,653 | 17,337 | 13,466 | – |
| Total operating expenses | 66,397 | 58,682 | 457,364 | 246,479 | 62,850 |
| | | | | | |
| Operating Income (Loss) | 18,978 | (12,936) | (426,341) | (190,048) | (54,907) |
| Operating margin | 17.6% | –20% | –827% | –199% | –249% |
| | | | | | |
| Gain on acquisition and dissolution of joint venture | 6,356 | 974 | 13,356 | | |
| Interest and other income | 1,342 | 1,106 | 3,221 | 2,252 | 1,978 |
| Income (loss) before income tax | 26,676 | (10,856) | (409,764) | (187,796) | (52,929) |
| Income tax provision | 1,891 | – | – | 1,810 | |
| Income (loss) from continuing operations | 24,785 | (10,856) | (409,764) | (189,606) | (52,929) |
| Discontinued operations: | | | | | |
| Loss from discontinued operations | (1,218) | (10,447) | (15,494) | – | – |
| Gain on sale of discontinued operations | 2,482 | – | – | – | – |
| Income (loss) from discontinued operations | 1,264 | (10,447) | (15,494) | – | – |
| Net income/loss | 26,049 | (21,303) | (425,258) | (189,606) | (52,929) |
| Net margin | 24% | –33% | –825% | –198% | –240% |

(continued)

| Table 9-1 | Ask Jeeves Inc. Consolidated Statement of Operations and Summary Balance Sheet Data, 1999–2003 (continued) |

| Summary Balance Sheet Data | (in thousands) | | | | |
|---|---|---|---|---|---|
| **At December 31** | **2003** | **2002** | **2001** | **2000** | **1999** |
| Cash and cash equivalents | 180,648 | 44,440 | 67,285 | 91,266 | 51,530 |
| Total current assets | 196,009 | 57,011 | 78,220 | 120,322 | 66,004 |
| Total assets | 212,255 | 72,176 | 111,338 | 537,867 | 75,764 |
| Total current liabilities | 23,721 | 42,573 | 62,327 | 68,210 | 30,647 |
| Total liabilities | 139,047 | 42,899 | 64,124 | 72,099 | 34,313 |
| Total stockholders' equity | 73,208 | 29,277 | 47,214 | 465,768 | 41,451 |

*Sources: Ask Jeeves Inc. Form 10-K for the fiscal year ended December 31, 2003, filed with the Securities and Exchange Commission on March 1, 2004; Ask Jeeves Inc. Form 10-K for the fiscal year ended December 31, 2002, filed with the Securities and Exchange Commission on March 12, 2003; Ask Jeeves Inc. Form 10-K for the fiscal year ended December 31, 2001, filed with the Securities and Exchange Commission on February 28, 2002.*

# FINANCIAL ANALYSIS

The overall financial picture of Ask Jeeves is that of a struggling Internet search company that has slowly been improving its financial performance over the last five years but has never shown a profitable year (Table 9-1).

The revenue picture of Ask Jeeves looks like a yo-yo trajectory that nevertheless points up. The company's revenues bolted from $22 million in 1999 to $95 million in 2000, only to plunge in the Internet advertising debacle of 2001 down to $51 million. By 2002, its revenues had recovered somewhat to $65 million, and in 2003, they increased significantly to $107 million. Net margins, which reached an all-time low of a negative 825% in 2001, have since also improved significantly, to a negative 33% in 2002, and then finally reaching a positive status in 2003, with a net margin of 24%. The wild swings in revenue have been caused by three factors. The top line revenues are highly sensitive to Internet advertising levels in general, which have been inconsistent. The company overspent on marketing in the first years, but has reduced those costs significantly to a more reasonable level of 30% of revenues in 2003. And foolish overpriced purchases in 2000 led to a huge write off of $355 million in 2001. With only around 300 employees, the company is highly leveraged in the context of the Internet economy in general. When times are good, this company does extraordinarily well. When times are bad, the company does not fare well.

An analysis of Ask Jeeves' revenue sources shows where its money is coming from (Table 9-2).

Paid placement revenue was up 136% in 2003, and clearly the money in Internet advertising is in paid placement for advertising provided by Ask Jeeves to advertisers and implemented through the DoubleClick network. Ask Jeeves has been late to the paid inclusion business, but in the first year it reaped nearly $1 million in revenues, and in 2003 increased that by over 150% to $2.3 million.

| Table 9-2 | Ask Jeeves Revenue Channels | | | | |
|---|---|---|---|---|---|
| | | | (thousands) | | |
| | 2003 | Change | 2002 | Change | 2001 |
| **Paid Placement** | | | | | |
| U.S. | $52,273 | 122% | $ 23,570 | 139% | $ 9,858 |
| Europe | 24,791 | 171% | 9,144 | | |
| Total | 77,064 | 136% | 32,714 | 231% | 9,858 |
| **Branded Advertising:** | | | | | |
| U.S. | 15,633 | (12.5%) | 17,875 | −19% | 22,296 |
| Europe | 7,732 | 5% | 7,349 | | |
| Total | 23,365 | (7%) | 25,224 | 13% | 22,296 |
| **Paid Inclusion** | | | | | |
| U.S. | 2,113 | 156.1% | 825 | | – |
| Europe | 225 | – | | | |
| Total | 2,338 | 183.4% | 825 | | – |
| Total | 102,767 | | 58,763 | −82.80% | 32,154 |

Source: Ask Jeeves Inc. Form 10-K for the fiscal year ended December 31, 2003, filed with the Securities and Exchange Commission on March 1, 2004.

The 2004 revenue picture looks quite bright for Ask Jeeves. In 2003, it achieved its first profitable year, focused on its core business by shedding its Web Solutions division, and extended its agreement with Doubleclick for an additional 3 years. In 2004, Ask Jeeves expects total revenues of between $220–$230 millon. It also raised over $110 million from the sale of convertible subordinated notes in June 2003, significantly bolstering its cash position. The company said it would use the proceeds of the notes for general corporate purposes and also for future acquisitions, and in March 2004, agreed to acquire Interactive Search Holdings, Inc., which operates the Excite.com and iWon.com portal sites, for $150 million in cash and 9.3 million shares of Ask Jeeves stock and options.

Looking at the Ask Jeeves balance sheet, total current assets declined over time from a high of $537 million in 2000 to $72 million in 2002, but has rebounded to $212 million at December 31, 2003. At December 31, the company also had $180 million in cash, enough to see it through a number of years of negative cash flow at the rate of $20 million a year. This increase is primarily attributable to its sale of convertible subordinated notes in June 2003, as noted above.

## STRATEGIC ANALYSIS: BUSINESS STRATEGIES

As the fifth largest player in Internet search, Ask Jeeves faces some difficult strategic issues. The most important issue is how it can differentiate itself from other search engines in a meaningful way. At a time when companies and audiences are consolidating into larger and larger entities, is there any room for a profitable niche player such as Ask Jeeves? Should it seek to be bought by Google or Yahoo! for a price based on the monetary value of its 30 million users?

In 2002, management focused on using new technologies to differentiate the company from other search engines. The technologies included scaling of the Teoma technology to support its traffic; integration of Teoma with prior search technologies; enhancement of search/retrieval technology for better relevance; knowledge-base development, including extension of existing natural language and knowledge-base techniques to improve relevance of search results and ad products; and data collection and database mining improvements, including expansion in the coverage of the data collection system to include all products and properties. In 2003, it continued those improvements, by introducing a set of intuitive search tools that it calls "Smart Search" and "Smart Product Search." Smart search tools provide the information the user seeks directly on the results page rather than providing links to sites that contain the information. Smart Product Search allows users to narrow their search results to include only products and services, and like Smart Search, also delivers its results directly to the results page.

## STRATEGIC ANALYSIS: COMPETITION

Of the nearly $1 billion spent on online search in the United States in 2003, Overture alone garnered $688 million, followed by Google ($294 million), Yahoo! ($140 million), MSN ($138 million), AOL ($92 million), LookSmart ($75 million), and finally Ask Jeeves ($74 million). The 2003 story of online search was that size of audience and reach counted most and this trend is likely to continue in 2004. Ask Jeeves competitors are busy combining and recombining into powerful search-content portal combinations that will be difficult to compete with. Yahoo! purchased Overture in 2003 and ended its relationship with Google. Combined with its earlier purchase of Inktomi, Yahoo! is poised to become the Web's premiere search/content site. MSN is developing its own paid-placement search engine technology, also combining search with content. In the competitive landscape, it appears that the big players are attempting to combine the functionality of a portal with a home-developed or -owned search engine, ending an earlier period when large portals would strike alliances with search engines and share the revenue. These alliances are dissolving, and portals with large audiences and more stable revenue streams are either buying search engines or developing their own. It will be difficult for pure search engines such as Ask Jeeves to survive alone as independents. A part of the elevated stock price of Ask Jeeves may well include its value as a buy-out candidate.

## STRATEGIC ANALYSIS: INFORMATION TECHNOLOGY

Ask Jeeves' computing infrastructure—like Google's—runs on inexpensive Intel-based servers. Ask Jeeves' Teoma search technology runs on arrays of Intel-based server systems running the Linux operating system and its natural language processing runs on arrays of Intel-based server systems running Microsoft Windows 2000 and Internet Information Server Software. The Question-Processing Engine, or QPE, is written in the C++ computer language and is optimized to handle high volumes. Ask Jeeves, like most search engines, can scale easily as user traffic increases by installing additional distribution servers. Its four Web sites are hosted by Metromedia Fibre Network in California and England, by Worldcom in Massachusetts, by Cable & Wireless Communications in England and by Esat Telecommunications in Ireland. The company maintains significant server over-capacity at each location so that if one hosting facility fails, another can service the entire user traffic.

## STRATEGIC ANALYSIS: SOCIAL AND LEGAL ISSUES

The company is not involved in significant litigation at this time. Ask Jeeves has been granted four United States patents, and it has eight patent applications pending for various aspects of its natural-language search and other database search technologies, which power the JeevesOne software product and the Ask.com Web site. The company has entered into an agreement with The Wodehouse No. 3 Trust concerning use of the Jeeves name and Butler logo. The Wodehouse No. 3 Trust is the successor to the late author, P. G. Wodehouse, the creator of the Jeeves character. The company makes quarterly payments to The Wodehouse No. 3 Trust. By its terms, the agreement is perpetual unless terminated by the company.

# FUTURE PROSPECTS

Although in the early years Ask Jeeves was successful in creating the market impression that it was easier to use and based its interface on so-called "natural language" parsing, by 2000 the development of search technology had bypassed Ask Jeeves. The legend is that in the early years, Ask Jeeves' natural language processors were really a crew of about 100 human editors who classified the incoming searches and Web sites into various categories and matched them by hand. Today it is difficult to assert that Ask Jeeves provides better search results than Google, which is based on pure popularity of Web sites, or Overture in delivering paid placement search results that simply require a bidding system. Lacking a technology edge, Ask Jeeves also lacks content and can make money only by passing users through to content or product destinations. Income from this source of advertising will become increasingly difficult as huge competitors such as Yahoo! and MSN vie for the same audience and as these sites garner ever larger shares of the Web audience. Ask Jeeves' management therefore faces a difficult future in their efforts to keep the company independent.

## SOURCES

Alterio, Julie Moran. "Ask Jeeves Buys Area Web Group." *The Journal News*, March 5, 2004.

Ask Jeeves Inc. Form 10-K for the fiscal year ended December 31, 2003, filed with the Securities and Exchange Commission on March 1, 2004.

Ask Jeeves Inc. Form 10-K for the fiscal year ended December 31, 2002, filed with the Securities and Exchange Commission on March 12, 2003.

Ask Jeeves Inc. Form 10-K for the fiscal year ended December 31, 2001, filed with the Securities and Exchange Commission on February 28, 2002.

Elgin, Ben. "Search Engines are Picking Up Steam." *BusinessWeek Online*, March 24, 2003.

Richmond, Riva. "Ask Jeeves Up 9.3%; Seen Gaining Leverage Over Google." Dow Jones News Wires, January 6, 2004.

Saranow, Jennifer. "Search Service Ask Jeeves Debuts New Online Shopping Topol." *Wall Street Journal*, November 4, 2003.

# RealNetworks:

## Media Player to Media Portal

RealNetworks is a leading provider of network-delivered media services and technology that enable digital media creation, distribution, and consumption. The company likes to think of itself as at the intersection between technology and content. The company has changed business plans and technologies several times as it has grown in a tumultuous Internet content world, competing against and allying itself with, at various times giants such as AOL/Time Warner and Microsoft. The company has developed three revenue streams: (1) electronic retailing of digital content to consumers, (2) provision of services to other businesses that want to distribute content over digital networks using RealNetworks' server software, and (3) supplying server-based software used by content owners and network operations to create and distribute digital content.

RealNetworks' leading product is called RealOne Player, which allows consumers to play, create, and manage digital media, rip and burn CDs, tune into Internet radio, and play streaming audio and video. Today more than 300 million people have registered to download RealOne Player, arguably the most widely distributed media player that is not built into an operating system. The basic version of RealOne is free, but more than 1 million paying consumers have signed up for a premium media service called RealOne SuperPass. Up until Apple Computer's iTunes network, RealNetworks had the largest paying subscription media base on the Internet, and today it is considered to be a model for other audio services. RealOne SuperPass users have access to content from content partners including CNN, Major League Baseball, NASCAR.com, and the *Wall Street Journal*.

RealNetworks employs about 340 people and in 2003 generated over $200 million in revenue with a net loss of $21 million. RealNetworks' stock price soared to nearly $100 in January 2000, but in spring 2004 is selling for about $6.50 a share.

## THE VISION

RealNetworks is one of the Internet's pioneers in the delivery and playback of streaming audio and visual programs on the Internet. RealNetworks was founded by people who got their training in media at Microsoft. In 1994, Rob Glaser left Microsoft, where he had been vice president of multimedia and consumer systems, to start the precursor to RealNetworks.

Glaser's original vision in 1994 was to build software and Web infrastructure (servers and client computers) that would permit millions of people to listen to online music and online videos by streaming files from Internet servers to remote client computers. While this idea is now commonplace, in 1994 the Internet was largely incapable of playing music or showing videos for three reasons: insufficient bandwidth to homes and offices, poor compression techniques, and slow hardware at both server and client levels. The idea of streaming media—as opposed to downloading entire videos or audio tracks—was appealing because it relied on moving small data packets across the Web rather than entire files; it therefore offered the possibility that even with the limited bandwidth of a telephone dial-up modem operating at 56 KBps, consumers could listen to music or view images. With RealAudio, the company's first product, Web users could view and hear content on demand without waiting hours or even days for large files to download.

The beginning of streaming began sometime during the ten-year period that Robert Glaser worked for Bill Gates at Microsoft. Glaser envisioned an infrastructure for delivering mass audiovisual multimedia content on the Web. Glaser left Microsoft and formed Progressive Networks in 1994 and in 1996 introduced Real Media Architecture, which uses very efficient encoding algorithms and produces relatively small files.

Originally the company focused on selling software (RealPlayer) that consumers could use to download, play, and catalog music files. By creating a viable platform for downloading music in the early years of the Internet, RealNetworks, along with Kazaa, Microsoft, and Apple, enabled and benefited from the massive explosion in music downloading. RealNetworks might have become the dominant player in Internet standards and software for playing music and video over the Internet were it not for Microsoft's monopoly of the desktop, its growing strength in corporate servers, and its decision to give away its own Windows Media Player. Worse, until recently, Microsoft programmed Windows XP to disable RealNetworks' software on installation and thereafter. In addition, until recently, Microsoft's XP operating system could not download music from the Web unless the consumer used Windows Media Player.

## BUSINESS MODEL

With Microsoft giving away its Media Player and giving away its content server as a part of the Windows 2000 Server operating system, RealNetworks was forced to innovate and develop new sources of revenue beginning in the late 1990s, when it became apparent that RealNetworks could easily suffer the fate of Netscape in its battles with Microsoft. In August 2000, RealNetworks began to change its business model from a software and infrastructure sales organization deriving revenues from the sale of its player into that of a consumer-oriented media portal, giving away a basic player and selling subscriptions to Web users who wanted online access to premium music, video, and news outlets. Once it succeeded in aggregating a significant online audience, it was able to sell access to that audience to advertisers (often media content companies such as CNN and major league sports teams). By selling access to its audience, RealNetworks has in part become an Internet advertising portal that aggregates audience by distributing digital content. In addition, it began to diversify into a business-to-business service company by creating a server media distribution platform called Helix, which it sells to large firms looking for a non-Microsoft server alternative for distributing audio and video content on corporate intranets as well as to broadband (DSL and cable) companies looking for a non-Microsoft server software to distribute content over their networks. RealNetworks derives about 40% of its total revenues from server licenses to corporations.

In each of these new areas of revenue generation, RealNetworks finds itself in direct competition with Microsoft, which is targeting the same markets. In December 2003, RealNetworks filed a $1 billion lawsuit in California against Microsoft for allegedly forcing PC manufacturers to include Windows Media Player as the default media player in return for allowing the manufacturers to install the Windows operating system. The European Commission has brought similar charges against Microsoft in Europe.

## FINANCIAL ANALYSIS

RealNetworks' revenue picture follows a roller-coaster pattern that reflects the competitive environment in which it operates, up one year, down one year and then up again (Table 10-1).

In 1999 and 2000, RealNetworks' pioneering technology dominated the marketplace. After 2000, the impact of competitors offering rival media players such as Microsoft's Media Player and Apple's Quicktime began to cut deeply into RealNetworks' revenues. Looking at the composition of revenues since 1999, software license fees peaked in 2000 and then have fallen in each year subsequent as corporations reduced information technology expenditures for content distribution servers. Advertising revenues also fell in this period to one-sixth their 2000 peak levels. The good news for RealNetworks is that service revenues derived from subscriptions and sales to consumers have more than doubled from 2000 to 2003 as the online music craze began to produce solid revenues from subscription services and software sales to consumers. Gross profit margins have declined each year since 2000 as the company made the transition to new products and services.

However, since 2000 the company has made real progress in improving its net margin (albeit still a negative number) from –46% in 2000 to –10.5% in 2003, and it has reduced annual losses from a high of $110 million in 2000 to $21 million in 2003. The company continues to spend a considerable amount on research and development, typical of an Internet software company. However, it has improved margins by reduced expenditures on advertising, personnel, and office facilities.

In general, the company's position improved in 2003 due almost entirely to its growth in the consumer market for subscriptions. Advertising revenue was flat, and sales of Helix to corporations suffered a 15% decline. Nevertheless,

| Table 10-1 | RealNetworks Consolidated Statements of Operations and Summary Balance Sheet Data, 1999–2003 |

| Consolidated Statements of Operations | | ( in thousands) | | | |
|---|---|---|---|---|---|
| **For the fiscal year ending December 31** | **2003** | **2002** | **2001** | **2000** | **1999** |
| **Net revenues** | | | | | |
| Software license fees | 61,970 | 72,753 | 108,586 | 148,091 | 90,627 |
| Service revenues | 134,058 | 103,161 | 64,740 | 52,505 | 26,466 |
| Advertising | 6,349 | 6,765 | 15,579 | 40,942 | 14,149 |
| Total net revenues | 202,377 | 182,679 | 188,905 | 241,538 | 131,242 |
| | | | | | |
| **Cost of revenues** | | | | | |
| Software license fees | 9,917 | 6,865 | 7,969 | 14,341 | 13,006 |
| Service revenues | 56,690 | 41,259 | 23,895 | 14,718 | 6,579 |
| Advertising | 1,736 | 2,145 | 6,324 | 9,629 | 2,906 |
| Total cost of revenues | 68,343 | 50,269 | 38,188 | 38,688 | 22,491 |
| **Gross profit** | **134,034** | **132,410** | **150,717** | **202,850** | **108,751** |
| **Gross margin** | **66%** | **72%** | **80%** | **84%** | **83%** |
| | | | | | |
| **Operating expenses** | | | | | |
| Research and development | 46,763 | 48,186 | 55,904 | 57,819 | 38,415 |
| Sales and marketing | 77,335 | 73,928 | 73,129 | 101,197 | 53,465 |
| General and administrative | 21,007 | 19,820 | 20,554 | 27,807 | 16,380 |
| Antitrust litigation | 1,574 | – | – | – | – |
| Loss on excess office facilities | 7,098 | 17,207 | 22,208 | – | – |
| Personnel reduction charges | – | 3,595 | 3,613 | – | – |
| Goodwill amortization, acquisitions charges, stock-based compensation | 1,120 | 1,328 | 40,633 | 142,053 | 3,531 |
| Total operating expenses | 145,897 | 164,064 | 216,041 | 328,876 | 111,791 |
| **Income (loss) from operations** | **(20,863)** | **(31,654)** | **(65,324)** | **(126,026)** | **(3,040)** |
| **Operating margin** | **−10%** | **−17%** | **−35%** | **−52%** | **−2%** |
| | | | | | |
| Other income (expense) | (444) | (727) | (13,497) | 18,871 | 9,966 |
| **Net income (loss)** | **(21,451)** | **(38,353)** | **(74,763)** | **(110,121)** | **6,926** |
| **Net margin** | **−10.5%** | **−21%** | **−40%** | **−46%** | **5%** |

**(continued)**

| Table 10-1 | RealNetworks Consolidated Statements of Operations and Summary Balance Sheet Data, 1999–2003 (continued) | | | | |
|---|---|---|---|---|---|
| **Summary Balance Sheet Data** | | | **(in thousands)** | | |
| **At December 31** | **2003** | **2002** | **2001** | **2000** | **1999** |
| Cash, cash equivalents and short-term investments | 373,593 | 309,071 | 344,509 | 364,710 | 344,627 |
| Working capital | 310,679 | 248,400 | 285,279 | 305,322 | 273,827 |
| Total assets | 580,939 | 462,101 | 567,860 | 578,408 | 411,124 |
| Total current liabilities | 82,411 | 74,509 | 77,553 | 82,801 | 80,565 |
| Total liabilities | 214,452 | 112,336 | 102,707 | 97,596 | 80,565 |
| Shareholders' equity | 366,487 | 349,765 | 464,879 | 480,812 | 330,559 |

*Sources: RealNetworks Form 10-K for the fiscal year 2003, filed with the Securities and Exchange Commission on March 15, 2004; RealNetworks Form 10-K for the fiscal year 2002, filed with the Securities and Exchange Commission on March 28, 2003.*

overall revenues increased about 10% year to year, and operating and net margins continued to improve. Net losses declined by about a third.

Looking at RealNetworks' balance sheet, the company remains in a strong financial position. With $373 million in cash and equivalents, the company has only $82 million in short-term obligations, a substantial reserve. The company could continue to cover losses at the current rate for many years.

# STRATEGIC ANALYSIS: BUSINESS STRATEGIES

Management has adopted two strategies in the past two years: (1) expand and enhance its premium content services, becoming more of a content music portal, and (2) fend off its major competitor by suing Microsoft for monopolistic behavior in the marketplace and joining with other technology firms competing with Microsoft in related markets, hoping to slow down Microsoft's efforts to become the single online media player. In April 2001, RealNetworks entered into a joint venture with media giants AOL Time Warner Inc., Bertelsmann AG, and EMI Group to create a platform for online music subscription services that used the RealOne media player. Called MusicNet, the service provides both a library of legally downloadable and streaming music.

In April 2003, RealNetworks acquired Listen.com, Inc. for $36 million. With this acquisition, RealNetworks owns two of the Internet's leading subscription content services—RealOne SuperPass and the Rhapsody music service (owned by Listen.com).

Rhapsody pioneered a number of important capabilities, such as integrating artist guides and customized radio stations within a music subscription service, and had its own streaming and caching technology. Listen.com has music assets that will enhance RealNetworks' music programming and provide operational efficiencies. Listen.com's distribution arrangements and technology partnerships with broadband cable and DSL providers, online music sites, computer manufacturers, and consumer electronics companies also will enhance the reach of RealNetworks' subscription offerings. Listen.com has distribution agreements with a network of more than 15 companies, including Time Warner Cable's Road Runner high-speed ISP, Charter Communications, Verizon Online, Sprint, Cablevision Systems Corporation's Optimum Online, Gateway, Lycos, RCN Corporation, and Sony's Musiclub.

With the addition of Rhapsody, RealNetworks has begun to aggressively acquire entire libraries of music and to move Rhapsody into more direct competition with Apple's iTunes competing music portal by offering legal songs for downloading and burning for 99 cents each. In August 2003, RealNetworks purchased the entire catalog of the Rolling Stones band for exclusive distribution through RealNetworks and Rhapsody. The Rolling Stones were one of several artist groups that had refused to release their music to legal Internet downloading sites, presumably because of the danger of widespread copying and loss of revenues to the artists. Also in August 2003, RealNetworks signed a distribution deal with consumer electronics giant Best Buy to sell its service at interactive kiosks in more than 560 stores throughout the United States. This move would be the first effort at integrating physical music stores with Web-based listening kiosks to support in-store sales. Prior to this agreement, it had always been assumed that physical music stores and Internet music stores were natural competitors, not strategic allies.

Management's other strategy is to attempt to slow the market penetration of Microsoft's Windows Media Player through legal actions taken with other firms or on its own. Since its inception, RealNetworks has stood directly in the crosshairs of Microsoft, which intends to dominate content distribution on the Internet. In its suit filed in December 2003, RealNetworks alleges that Microsoft is using its control of the desktop and business server markets to restrict consumer choice by preventing RealNetworks' RealOne media player from being installed on new PCs by manufacturers through exclusive licensing agreements.

## STRATEGIC ANALYSIS: COMPETITION

Although RealNetworks was a pioneer in developing the technology of audio streaming, it has not been able to turn its first-mover status into a permanent advantage. Instead, it faces competition on both the technology and content fronts. In technology, Microsoft, Apple Computer, AOL/Time Warner, Yahoo!, Netscape, and others have developed proprietary content-streaming software that is competitive with RealOne features. In terms of exclusive content, RealNetworks competes with existing subscription portals that have much larger audiences—such as Yahoo! and MSN—each of which can aggregate very large audiences and can afford to pay for music content if they do not already own large music libraries like AOL/Time Warner.

In addition to these legal competitors, RealNetworks faces significant competition with free illegal services such as Kazaa and Morpheus, among many others.

## STRATEGIC ANALYSIS: TECHNOLOGY

RealNetworks faces a number of technology challenges. To some extent the story of this company is all about technology. It no longer maintains a firm leading-edge grip on content distribution technology given all its competitors. In some cases, Microsoft's operating systems have been known to block or change user settings, preventing the operation of the RealOne Player. Although the continuing deployment of broadband represents an opportunity for the company, it is also a threat. Broadband companies—DSL and cable—are developing their own music distribution services and technologies. The fastest growth in online access is occurring not with PCs but with other devices, such as cell phones, PDAs, game consoles, set-top boxes, Internet appliances, and interactive television. In these non-PC areas, RealNetworks will have to convince manufacturers to install the RealOne player.

## STRATEGIC ANALYSIS: SOCIAL AND LEGAL CHALLENGES

The company at this time does not face any significant social and legal challenges against it. RealNetworks has been a strong supporter of legally downloading music and has taken a strong stand in defending record labels and artists against the threat of illegal copying and distribution on the Internet.

## FUTURE PROSPECTS

Management will clearly have to focus on growing the subscription business for legal online content. Here it will be assisted by the growing legal efforts of the recording industry to sue large-scale violators of copyright laws. The future of the company will depend on the ability of management to develop alliances with content owners (bands and artists), content portals such as AOL, Yahoo!, and MSN, and manufacturers looking for non-Microsoft ways to offer content to their customers. For instance, on January 15, 2004, Time Warner Cable and RealNetworks announced that Time Warner Cable was licensing the company's RealMedia delivery platform and Helix media delivery software and application software to support Road Runner, Time Warner Cable's high-speed data service. Time Warner Cable will deploy Helix Universal Servers throughout their network to manage Time Warner Cable's Internet media and to efficiently and reliably deliver a large volume of high-quality streaming audio and video content to Road Runner high-speed data customers. Time Warner, which competes with Microsoft on many fronts, is an ideal partner for RealNetworks.

To strengthen its content offerings to consumers and leverage its music investments, RealNetworks purchased in January 2004 Seattle-based GameHouse, Inc., a top developer, publisher, and distributor of downloadable PC games, in a transaction valued at approximately $35.6 million. The acquisition strengthens RealNetworks' leadership position in the downloadable PC games market by bringing together RealArcade, a leading downloadable games distribution platform, and GameHouse, a major developer and publisher of downloadable games. This acquisition contributes to RealNetworks' overall strategy to be the leading provider of digital media consumer services.

While the future holds many opportunities in each of the areas described, there is also strong competition. RealNetworks is in a weak position currently vis-à-vis two competitors: Apple and Microsoft. Apple can afford to sell music for 99 cents a song in part because users of iTunes have to purchase a $300 Apple iPod listening device. Likewise, Microsoft can afford to offer its players, servers, and even content for next to nothing because users will have to purchase a Windows operating system. But RealNetworks has no complimentary technology product and therefore must rely on the content alone to produce revenues and profits.

## SOURCES

Black, Jane. "The Stones' New Tune: Start Me Up, Digitally." *BusinessWeek Online*, August 18, 2003.

DeCarlo, Lisa, and Arik Hesseldahl. "RealNetworks Files Suit Against Microsoft." Forbes.com, December 19, 2003.

Lohr, Steve. "Musical Chairs with the Big Boys." *The New York Times*, March 21, 2004.

RealNetworks Form 10-K for the fiscal year 2003, filed with the Securities and Exchange Commission on March 15, 2004.

RealNetworks Form 10-K for the fiscal year 2002, filed with the Securities and Exchange Commission March 28, 2003.